High Tickets Remote Closing

Building Relations & Closing Deals

RCA Warrior Max Steel

© Copyright 2024 - All rights reserved.

The content contained within this book may not be reproduced, duplicated or transmitted without direct written permission from the author or the publisher.

Under no circumstances will any blame or legal responsibility be held against the publisher, or author, for any damages, reparation, or monetary loss due to the information contained within this book, either directly or indirectly.

Legal Notice:

This book is copyright protected. It is only for personal use. You cannot amend, distribute, sell, use, quote or paraphrase any part, or the content within this book, without the consent of the author or publisher.

Disclaimer Notice:

Please note the information contained within this document is for educational and entertainment purposes only. All effort has been executed to present accurate, up to date, reliable, complete information. No warranties of any kind are declared or implied. Readers acknowledge that the author is not engaged in the rendering of legal, financial, medical or professional advice. The content within this book has been derived from various sources. Please consult a licensed professional before attempting any techniques outlined in this book.

By reading this document, the reader agrees that under no circumstances is the author responsible for any losses, direct or indirect, that are incurred as a result of the use of the information contained within this document, including, but not limited to, errors, omissions, or inaccuracies.

Introduction

Finally, allow me to welcome you to the world of remote closing of high-ticket deals, known as 'high-ticket remote closing' online. Learning and mastering this field is the best decision of your life, and this book will prepare you for a successful start. Written as the ultimate handbook for every salesperson and team leader, it acts as a dependable and fully detailed guide that will give you the key skills, strategies and tools you need for success.

Why High-Ticket Remote Closing?

Creating a remote closing side business focusing on high-ticket items will likely be the most profitable skill set you amass in your entire career because high ticket items live in a world of their own, and they're completely different from the normal day-to-day sales filth geared toward meaningless consumerism.

 Not only are you selling things for drastically higher price points than 99 per cent of salespeople will ever touch, but you're also selling entirely different kinds of things – things such as software, coaching, training and expanding lines of credit up to or over $100,000. Individual high-ticket sales can be much larger contracts and often take longer to negotiate, close, onboard and placate, while still getting the results you agreed upon in the beginning. Simply put, high ticket items require different sales skills when compared with the norms of everyday sales. They require a deep and wide-ranging knowledge of buyer psychology, advanced closing techniques and a dedicated approach that forges a strong relationship built on trust with your clientele. That's why remote closing – whether you're closing high-ticket deals from a beachfront bungalow in Bali or hanging from a jungle hammock in Central America, while your prospective clients are in a face-to-face setting – is an opportunity that's nearly impossible to come by, and definitely won't be around for long if you ever want to create a six-figure side business from your home, which requires nothing but a mobile phone and a wi-fi connection.

What You'll Learn

The book is built to take you through step-by-step the practice of high-ticket remote closing, ensuring you learn correctly. Each chapter builds on the previous one, keeping things seamless and comprehensive throughout. Here's what you'll find:

Laying The Foundations Of High-Ticket Sales:

Discover what high-ticket sales are, how they can help your business, and what you need to know to succeed.

The Psychology of Buying:

Understand the psychology behind buyer decisions and motivations, including how to build buyer trust and when to abandon trust so as not to be scammed. Psychology of Selling: Find out how to identify and activate different psychological triggers in potential buyers, leading to increased sales and faster purchases.

Essential Sales Skills:

Matters such as active listening, how to be an effective communicator and an advanced negotiator.

Sales Tools:

Consider the digital tools that speed up your sales cycle from start to finish, including CRM systems, video conferencing, analytics tools and more.

The sales process (structured steps to acquire leads, strike deals, and maintain relationships after the sale) can provide structure.

Advanced Techniques:

Learn proven high-ticket sales techniques such as value-based selling, solution selling and using case studies.

Client Relationships:

Build and maintain strong client relationships through personalized communication and consistent follow-up.

Closing Strategies:

Discover various closing techniques tailored for high-pressure situations and high-ticket deals.

Overcoming Objections:

Equip yourself with strategies to handle objections and turn them into opportunities.

Case Studies:

Draw useful insights from victories already achieved where your poster can start to captivate professionals and general public alike Courtesy the author.

Personal Growth:

Fulfil your potential through a growth mindset, reach for personal goals and strive for a productive work/life balance.

Industry Insights:

tailor your emails based on the industry you work in, eg real estate, tech etc

Lead Generation:

Implement effective lead generation strategies using content marketing, social media, and more.

Crafting the Perfect Pitch:

Perfect your pitch to engage and persuade high-ticket clients.

How to Scale Your Business:

Build a sales team, automate and grow efficiently.

Metrics and Analytics: Use data-driven decision-making to track performance and refine your strategies.

Second is networking and community building:

create a robust professional network to facilitate selling and investing; also become part of a community of investors, who can share resources, increase your knowledge base and positively impact your growth.

Future Trends:

Understand the next wave of trends affecting remote closing – from artificial intelligence (AI) and automation to changes in buyer behaviour.

My Journey

I've been in remote high-ticket closing – either acting as a close or working for a company with remote closing – for quite some time. My voyage into the world of high-ticket, remote closing began when I began selling traditional, in-person F2F or B2B type sales. However, the unique benefits of remote working and selling high-ticket gear convinced me to give it a try. Over time, my calls have gotten better, I've kept up with technology, and I've learned from successes and failures. The lessons in this book are lessons learned from the experiences noted above. These recommendations are things that I impart to my own clients so that they can successfully build and sustain a career in remote high-ticket closing.

Your Journey Starts Here

As is the case with most things worth learning, tapping into this world means you are going to have to bring yourself to the table, willing to learn, and ready to take action. High-ticket remote closing isn't just about closing deals with other people, it's about building relationships, generating value, and becoming a better version of yourself. I hope that as you move through each chapter, you'll take the time to reflect on what you're learning, practice the techniques you pick up and see how they shape your context and ultimately your performance. This book was originally published in 2020 by the author and is republished here with permission.

Remote sales are the future. High-ticket, high-value, and largely about relationship and technology. If you can master high-ticket remote closing, you're at the cutting edge of this evolution. You're going to break through your own personal ceiling by learning how to trade high-ticket, remote. You're going to break through your own career ceiling and nobody else is teaching this stuff. Nobody else. It's going to be a very special, powerful, incredible personal journey for you.

Here's to your success!

Chapter 1:

Introduction to High-Ticket Remote Closing

"Success in high-ticket sales begins with understanding the value you bring and the trust you build."

-Someone that we don't know

1.1 Definition and Importance

Welcome to the world of high-ticket remote closing. You could sell high-priced products or services online such as digital information products or coaching services. They're usually valued at $1,000 or more and clients never see you or meet with you in person – you can place orders and pay for them online. To sell and close in this model you use online digital tools like video conferencing, CRM software, email, and others.

Why should you care? Because the world of business is changing. Thanks to the rise of the internet, the majority of companies are now endeavoring to do what they used to do in their offices in the wilds of Wisconsin or walk-ups in Auckland: pitch, provide cover, maintain contact, move and merge. And do it from anywhere. That's the secret and the future of remote closing – it's just not a fad, an option, or a special case but more of a next-generation way to make the sale with endless possibilities: anytime, anywhere.

1.2 Benefits of High-Ticket Sales

High-ticket sales come with a host of benefits:

- **Higher Income**: Close less to make more. It's simple math: sell a few high-ticket items and watch your income skyrocket.

- **Premium Clients**: By setting performance and image targets combined with charging appropriately high rates you can attract clients (a) who appreciate and value the additional benefits you provide and (b) who are willing to pay for them.

- **Reputation Builders**: Just like any business, although your primary purpose will be selling directly to clients, look for partners who will recommend your services and spread the word about the benefits of your work to their friends and networks.

- **Deep Relationships**: Build stronger, long-term relationships with clients who are invested in your success.

- **Career Development**: Gain experience in handling large sales together with training to become a top-notch sales professional.

- **Work Flexibility**: You set your own hours and work anywhere. 100% cubicle-free.

- **Consumer Naturalism**: Synaesthesia Club is producer-driven—no retail mark-up!

- **Advisory Boards**: We sell one-time peripherals to gadgets giving you control over what you purchase.

1.3 Overview of the Book Structure

Here's a sneak peek at what's in store:

- **Chapter 1**: Introduction to High-Ticket Remote Closing
- **Chapter 2**: The Psychology of Buying
- **Chapter 3**: Essential Sales Skills
- **Chapter 4**: Mastering Digital Tools
- **Chapter 5**: The Sales Process
- **Chapter 6**: High-Ticket Sales Techniques
- **Chapter 7**: Building and Maintaining Client Relationships
- **Chapter 8**: Overcoming Objections
- **Chapter 9**: Scaling Your Business
- **Chapter 10**: Metrics and Analytics
- **Chapter 11**: Personal Development and Mindset
- **Chapter 12**: Future Trends in Remote Closing

Each chapter brims with nuggets of helpful advice, case studies from real practice, and enough humor to keep things entertaining. Here we go.

1.4 Key Concepts to Master

While we're at it, here are a couple of definitions that you'll need to master:

- **Lead Generation**: Finding potential clients who are interested in your product or service.

- **Qualification**: Determining whether a lead is a good fit for your offer.

- **Building Relationships**: Creating strong connections with your clients based on trust and mutual benefit.

- **Closing**: The final step where you seal the deal and make the sale.

These are what make up high-ticket remote closing. Get good at these and you're already half-done.

1.5 Setting Expectations

Don't get me wrong, remote closing isn't easy – it takes effort, stamina, and continuous education and adaptation – but if you're willing to take a shot at it, it's great practice.

You are in for longer sales cycles and more complicated buying cycles – but your payouts will be higher and the customer relationships will be better.

1.6 Common Misconceptions

Let's debunk some myths, shall we?

- **Myth #1**: Remote closing is easier than traditional sales.
    - **Reality**: It's more fluid but less flexible.

- **Myth #2**: You need to be a tech wizard.
    - **Reality**: Basic tech skills are all you really need. The tools are easy to use – we'll walk you through them.
- **Myth #3**: It's all about the pitch.
    - **Reality**: Building relationships and understanding client needs are just as important.

Remote closing is a hybrid of art and science. You must be both techno-savvy and people-savvy and a strategy master to boot.

1.7 Required Tools and Resources

To succeed in remote closing you'll need a few essential tools:

- **CRM Software**: To manage your leads and client interactions (think Salesforce, HubSpot).
- **Video Conferencing Tools**: For virtual meetings and presentations (Zoom, Microsoft Teams).
- **Email Management Systems**: To keep your communications organized (Gmail with Boomerang, Outlook).
- **Messaging Apps**: For quick, real-time communication (Slack, WhatsApp).

These tools will be your best friends, helping you stay organized and efficient.

1.8 Summary and Objectives

By the end of this chapter, you should have a solid understanding of:

- What high-ticket remote closing is and why it's important.
- The benefits of aiming for high-ticket sales.
- The structure and key concepts of this course.

- Realistic expectations and common misconceptions.

- The essential tools and resources needed for success.

Ready to dive deeper? Let's go!

1.9 The Evolution of Sales

A generation ago, the sales profession might have involved knocking on someone's door to sell an encyclopedia set or making 'inbound calls' to ensure that everybody in the Yellow Pages took out an eye-catching new ad. Today the global marketplace is so multi-channel and multi-modal that digital technologies facilitate the closing of deals without any personal contact with a customer ever being necessary. In chasing that needle, the profession of sales is going through a radical transformation.

Face-to-face interactions are no longer the go-to. Instead, remote closings rely on digital conversations, data modeling, and personal communication to put people over the line. Catching up with our future in sales should be at the top of anyone's to-do list.

1.10 The Impact of Technology

Technology really is the enabler of remote closing. From your customer relationship management (CRM) system that enables you to manage all your sellers' interactions to video conferencing software that allows you to meet face-to-face, it is technology that has changed the way we sell, how we sell, and to whom we sell. Here's how:

- **Automation**: Automate repetitive tasks to focus on high-value activities.

- **Data Analytics**: Use data to understand client behavior and tailor your approach.

- **Communication Tools**: Connect with clients through multiple channels—email, video, messaging.

- **Social Media**: Leverage platforms like LinkedIn to generate leads and build relationships.

You can't avoid technology, so you might as well get comfortable with these tools. The more comfortable you are, the better remotely you can close the deal.

1.11 The Role of the Internet

Remote closing relies entirely on the internet – if it wasn't for the web, none of this would work. Here's why it's so crucial:

- **Global Reach**: Connect with clients from all over the world.

- **Information Access**: Research clients and tailor your pitch based on their needs.

- **Marketing Channels**: Utilize SEO, content marketing, and social media to generate leads.

- **Online Presence**: Build a professional online presence that attracts clients and builds trust.

If you honestly want to land your next dream job, the biggest tool available to you presently is the internet. Use it as fiercely as you possibly can.

1.12 Future of Remote Closing

Remote closing is definitely here to stay. As businesses embrace digital transformation, the need for capable, qualified remote closers will grow too. Here are a few trends to keep in mind:

- **AI and Automation**: The use of Artificial Intelligence will continue to increase (e.g., in lead generation and client management and also in how we analyze our data).

- **Personalization**: Personalized marketing and sales approaches will become the norm.

- **Virtual Reality**: VR could revolutionize product demos and client meetings.

- **Sustainability**: Travel fewer miles (and have a lower carbon footprint) by selling off-site remotely.

You'll stay ahead of them and remain competitive and effective as remote sales become commonplace.

Conclusion

The world of high-ticket remote closing is a great place to be. It is fast-paced, exciting, and full of opportunity for those who are willing to learn and adjust. Leading a remote sales team and delivering on the highest level requires mastering technology and tapping into human psychology.

Get ready to boss the world of high-ticket remote closing and move your sales career to another level. Throughout this acclaimed book, you will learn the techniques, tools, skills, and knowledge to be the best and be confident for the big moments.

In the next step, we'll touch on buying psychology and examine what makes people buy the high-ticket items. Read on!

Chapter 2:

The Psychology of Buying

"People buy emotionally and justify logically." - Zig Ziglar

2.1 Understanding Buyer Motivation

Welcome to the mind of your buyer! Understanding what drives people to make high-ticket purchases is definitely an important part of that equation. As it turns out, intrinsic and extrinsic forms of motivation can be viewed as the two primary driving forces for any kind of human action – not just those of a spending nature.

- **Intrinsically Motivated**: This comes from the individual buyer. The buyer feels good about herself: she is going after her life goals, she is working on a real need, and her purchase is going to satisfy her own desires. For example, maybe she wants to perform better during her workouts or she wants to flatten her stomach for a trip to the beach. I once had a client who bought a platinum online learning course as she wanted to switch jobs and needed training in the new skills.

- **External Rewards and Punishments**: These include social esteem, reward, or avoiding punishment in other ways. For example, buying a luxury car to gain recognition from others. Another client of mine purchased a high-ticket business coaching package to 'gain respect' in her industry.

Understanding what motivates your buyers also equips you to adapt your sales pitch to appeal to their motivations. For example, if your prospect is motivated by mastery, emphasize how your product can help them reach their goals. If your prospect is motivated by social status, highlight client testimonials about how the product enhances their social status.

2.2 Emotional vs. Rational Purchases

Often our purchases are a mix of emotion and reason. High-priced and high-prestige purchases in general pull on the emotion strings, but even lower-priced items follow this pattern. Consider how many feelings we have about making purchases.

- **Emotional Purchases**: Made due to emotional states including desire, fear, joy, pride. For example, desire for status might fuel an expensive watch purchase, while joy might fuel the purchase of a luxury retreat when under stress. (One client purchased a luxury retreat to seek joy in their life during a hard time.)

- **Rational Purchases**: Guided by rational and objective thoughts pertaining to the purchase such as price, features/benefits, etc. When a software solution is selected upon a cost-benefit analysis of the number of people it would serve and the appropriate cost-benefit ratio, it is a logical, rational, and objective purchase. The software solution selected by the tech company of which I was a part was a high-ticket software package chosen after a clear cost per employee and other efficiency improvement ROI had been carried out.

Understanding the proper balance between the emotional and rational factors will help you structure your sales pitch in a way that is likely to resonate with both. If your prospect is largely emotionally driven, tell stories that appeal to the emotional benefits; for a prospect who is largely rational, pitch facts and figures and focus on data and logic.

2.3 The Decision-Making Process

The decision-making process for high-ticket purchases typically involves several stages:

1. **Awareness**: The prospect becomes aware of a need or problem. (Typically the role of your marketing efforts.) 'Amazing what Facebook ads can do' I said to myself after running some targeted ads that created awareness that there were even challenges that my product addressed.

2. **Evaluation**: The buyer weighs different solutions. To go beyond top-of-mind recall here, you have to build real trust and give prospects relevant and useful information. I like to provide robust guides and demos.

3. **Decision**: The buyer chooses a solution and buys it. That's the reason why strong value proposition and trust are important right here. I make sure my clients feel confident and knowledgeable about their decision.

4. **Post-Purchase**: The buyer evaluates their decision. After-sales support and care help clients feel successful, which lays the foundation for a long-term relationship. I'll check back in with clients regularly and provide other resources.

Each stage needs a nuanced approach to get the consumer to the next stage; such as in the awareness stage, you might focus on the problem your product solves, and in the decision stage, you focus on the benefits that are a unique feature of your solution.

2.4 The Role of Trust in Sales

Trust is the cornerstone of any successful sales relationship, particularly for those of us in high-ticket sales. When there is no trust involved, there ceases to be any real commitment from the buyer.

- **Trust**: Be consistent, transparent, reliable. Be on time, do what you say, and be as transparent as you can about your product – what it does and just as importantly what it doesn't do. For me, this involves following up with an email several days after my first meeting or call summarizing our key points of discussion and underscoring how my product specifically addresses their identified pain point.

- **Trust**: Talk, be open and honest, provide great customer service, address issues that come up. An early client used the software I was building, and she realized she had technical difficulties. Immediate responsiveness and having a great support team resulted in building that person as a great client and someone who has referred us to others.

Case Study: Emma's Trust-Building Strategy
Notably, the best remote closers all followed up afterward with emails summarizing the key takeaways from their meetings and emphasizing how the product addressed those needs. Emma, a top remote closer, was adamant about this stage. 'You have to be there [emotionally and mentally] to respond if they follow up,' she said. 'Or at the very least you have to send an email confirming the next steps and the issues that were solved. That's how you establish trust. And they need that reassurance that you're professional and you follow through on your responsibilities.'

2.5 Identifying Customer Pain Points

In order to make higher-ticket sales, you need to identify the customer pain points; put simply, what is causing your clients' frustration or problems? Pain points are the moment when something starts to go wrong.

- **Pain Points**: There are various types – financial (can be about saving money), productivity-related (improvement of efficiency), process-related (simplifying workflows), or personal (improvement of a career, reduction of stress).

- **Pain Points**: Identify the problems clients might have. Find out by asking them what their pain points are. As a consultant, I will always ask: 'What is your biggest challenge in your business right now?'

Once a pain point is presented, tailor your closer towards that pain. If a client expresses a pain point of productivity, tout how your solution can eliminate time and consolidate his processes.

2.6 The Influence of Social Proof

Social proof is an established psychological cue that can have a powerful effect on spending decisions. Mimicry is a fascinating phenomenon, especially in places where there are lots of people. When you're not sure what to do, your tendency is to look around at others and do what they're doing.

- **Types of Social Proof**: Testimonials, case studies, reviews, and endorsements from industry experts.

- **With Social Proof**: Building your case by quoting experts and social proof: 'As the American entrepreneur Andrew Carnegie once said

"90 percent of all millionaires became so through ownership of real estate."' A good image will make it much more useful! Demonstrating social proof – in other words, how your company has made a difference on the ground by quoting from vetted clients and so on – is a winning strategy. In my presentation, I insert videos with the voices of clients who are happy about the results of our collaboration.

For example, maybe you include the case study of a previous client who got incredible results so that your prospect can imagine how that sort of result could work for them too. It's a proven psychological fact that case studies of previous clients work like a magnet in pulling prospects toward making the purchase. It's powerful credibility and interest – if our prospect sees that you've helped someone else get great results, they think to themselves, well maybe I can get similar results too. In fact, one of my prospects was imagining how that other client had doubled their revenue in six months using the steps outlined in my blueprint 30 minutes prior to contacting me.

2.7 Building Buyer Personas

Buyer personas are semi-fictional representations of your ideal customer based on real data and research. They serve as a representation of your target market and help you better understand your buyers so you can personalize content and better market to and sell to prospects.

- **Demographics**: Job role, challenges, goals, buying behavior, preferred communication channels.

- **Build Buyer Personas**: Interview current customers, examine current sales, and comb through your customer interactions to gather as much data as possible on the people experiencing your products and make the persona (it's like a three-dimensional online profile explaining the psychology of your ideal customer) that reflects them as humans. For example, one of my clients I send out

~20-question surveys every several months because the more I know about them, the more I can help them to understand what they truly want.

Knowing your buyer personas means you can create a sales persona that 'fits' that specific segment of your audience. It could be a search-oriented, tech-savvy executive, a small-business owner who is time-poor, or a marketing team that requires hands-on interaction.

2.8 Tailoring Your Approach

There is no one-size-fits-all in high-ticket. Customize to each prospect and have the mindset of 'shake and take' – Daniel Woodward, The Value Factory

- **Personalize**: Tailor your pitch and presentation to the prospect's industry, role, and needs. For example, if pitching a healthcare provider, emphasize features related to patient care and practice efficiency.

- **Value Proposition**: Clearly spell out what the product or service you're selling will do for the prospect as it relates to the channels, goals, and obstacles you learned about while taking notes and listening to the client.

Case Study: David's Tailored Sales Pitch
He was a great remote closer because he always did his homework tailoring a pitch to a prospect's needs by using features that were most relevant to his or her business – a tactic that led to greater engagement and therefore to more closes. Once writing to a software buyer at a logistics company with thousands of trucks to manage, David led with features that made clear how his solution could streamline their supply-chain activities.

2.9 Overcoming Buyer Hesitation

Hesitation can be common in a high-ticket purchase since it's such a big commitment, so it's important to understand it and overcome them to push the deal forward.

- **Regular Excuses**: 'Costs too much.' 'I don't like change.' 'Don't trust the vendors.' 'I don't know how I'll get ROI.'

- **Dealing with Hesitation**: Be able to provide detail, offer demonstrations or allow a test run, share stories of people who have used it successfully, account for the cost (what you'll get for it, what it costs other people), and the benefits. A free trial period, for instance, can ease the fear of making a bad investment.

With another client who had concerns about making a financial investment into my high-ticket coaching program, I was able to allay their fears by giving them a dollar-for-dollar breakdown of anticipated return on investment, pulling in previous testimonials from clients, and offering an installment payment plan.

2.10 Psychological Triggers

Psychological triggers can dramatically move a prospect towards buying – and if you have a high ticket product to sell, they can give you just what you need to make the sale. Here are a few coming up:

- **The Insider / Outsider Trigger**

- **The Authority / Expert Trigger**

- **The Social Proof Trigger**

- **The Short Term Loss – Long Term Gain Trigger**

- The Time Limited Offer Trigger
- The Scarcity Trigger
- The Ultimatum Trigger
- The Reciprocation Trigger
- The Commitment and Consistency Trigger
- The Unity Trigger

Now let's look at just a couple of them.

- **Scarcity**: Try pointing out that there are limited spots left in your premium coaching programme, for example.
- **Authority**: You can build credibility by referencing expertise in your field and by getting other trusted figures to endorse you. I quote a range of respected industry experts who have had good experiences of my work.
- **Reciprocity**: A prospect might feel naturally obligated to repay you in some way if you offer something of value. A free lead magnet (such as an eBook or webinar) might create goodwill.
- **Commitment**: Get them to commit to something small or low risk now (e.g.: mailing list) in order to increase the likelihood they will buy something bigger later (e.g.: high-ticket product).

Using these triggers ethically and effectively can enhance your sales strategy.

2.11 Creating Urgency

Adding urgency can push prospects towards a decision before they've had a chance to doubt, procrastinate, or ignore the offer.

- **Urgency-Inducing Tactics**: Time-limited offers, special deals limited to a specific time, highlighting the cost of doing nothing (Example: This discount is available just this week).

- **Keeping the Pressure and Urgency in Balance**: Urgency is only helpful once it is kept on the right side of the precarious duplex void that is as a motivation to act now fully understood as highlighting the advantages of acting now, but not so much hurry to become pressure. For example, 'don't miss out on this special offer, almost gone, last chance.' Urgency turned into pressure where the receiver feels the pressure to act rather than the advantage of acting. I always make sure that my urgency messages are charged in a way that leads to motivation for action on the benefits side of the void and not on the pressure side.

For example, offering a discount on your service for the next 48 hours or showing how your product will solve an immediate problem creates a sense of urgency. One year, I offered a discount for year-end consulting services. It forced several clients to sign on before the offer expired.

2.12 Understanding Buyer's Remorse

Buyer's remorse is the regret or anxiety buyers may feel after making a purchase, especially an expensive one. Addressing this proactively can lead to higher customer satisfaction and loyalty.

- **Manage Buyer's Remorse**: Set realistic expectations, provide a meaningful pre-sale and post-sale support system (and follow up for six months to address any issues). I always have an after-sale conversation with my clients to check in a week after the purchase to make sure they're satisfied with their decision.

Example: Checking in with a customer a few days after the sale to ensure they have everything they need and aren't experiencing buyer's remorse shows that you are interested in their happiness and will be there to support them after the onboarding process.

Conclusion

To be a rockstar at high-ticket remote closing, you must have a background in the psychology of buying. You need to know how your audience thinks, what motivates them into action, and how to overcome further objections and close the deal.

Now let's jump into the top skills needed for mastering high-ticket remote closing: Go!

Chapter 3: Essential Sales Skills

"THE ART OF COMMUNICATION IS THE LANGUAGE OF LEADERSHIP." - JAMES HUMES

3.1 Active Listening

What's active listening? It's not just hearing words; it's really perceiving what your client says and needs and is an important skill for the remote closer.

- **What It Is**: With active listening, you focus, understand, respond, and then you remember what the client said; you both hear the emotions underlying the words, not just the words themselves.

- **Why It Matters**: Not only is a calmer and more patient therapist better able to uncover her clients' true needs, she can do so in a way that fosters even better communication. When we hear other people out and really listen to them, we extend more trust and respect to them. Therefore, they're more willing to trust us and the guidance we give them.

- **How to Do It**: Look at the camera (or person on the other end of the screen), nod along to show that you're taking in what they say, and yes, repeat back what they say at times so that you show that you did indeed understand what they said. Ask clarifying questions but also don't interrupt.

For example, while I was on a sales call, a client mentioned his apprehensions about the investment in a costly service. Once identified, this apprehension was connected to the underlying fear of not getting a satisfactory return on their investment. After I shared specific success stories and shared detailed ROI calculations, his fears were quelled and hence the sale was made.

3.2 Effective Communication

Professionals who have achieved financial success build their sales business on the foundation of effective communication: be clear, get to the point, and engage.

- **Dejargonise**: Say what you want to say in no fancier language than you need to. Don't cloak your meaning with obscure terminology. 'If you can't simply and fearlessly say what you really want to say to your audience without feeling flustered or melting into a pile of jargon, you are better not saying it at all.' Your dear client won't have the time or inclination to stroll thoughtfully through a labyrinth of complex terminology and still have the chance to respond to your overture. Say what you want to say in the simplest language possible.

- **Demonstrate Transparency**: If you need to use special terms, provide an explanation that's as clear as possible. If what you have to say is too complex for a simple paragraph, then try using a well-selected metaphor or analogy.

- **Be Concise**: Simple is often better – don't overwhelm your clients with information. Be direct and brief. Don't ramble on with non-essential information. Stay on track with the most important points you have in your manuscript that address the needs of the client.

- **Invitation**: Speak conversationally, ask questions, engage, and draw the client into the dialogue. Use stories and examples to make your points more visceral.

For example, I had one prospect who was overwhelmed with detailed specifications about a product. By dialing my language down and changing the focus from 'here's what it does' to 'here's what it does for you,' I was also able to bring the focus down to their business, narrowing their vision and getting us to the sale. The analogies I used were all borrowed from their industry. The benefits became more easy to make and therefore more compelling.

3.3 Negotiation Techniques

Negotiation is a skill for fostering a give-and-take situation in which you and your client both come out on top.

- **Preparation**: Learn as much as you can about your product, the market, and the client. This enables you to get to the 'fair' ie most advantageous result. Find out about your client's business and their likely objections.

- **Flexibility**: Be ready to bend – sometimes an extra perk or slippage can help close the gap.

- **Confidence**: Make your case with confidence and if the terms don't meet your minimum objectives, be prepared to walk away. Confidence can make the client feel like their decision was solid.

For example, in one negotiation where a client wanted a cheaper price for a premium-end consulting package, I was able to offer extra services as part of the deal which helped everyone reach an agreement and get value without undermining or devaluing the core offering. This demonstrated my flexibility and desire to be a true collaborator which helped to reinforce the client relationship.

3.4 Persuasion Strategies

Persuasion is about influencing a client's decision by presenting compelling arguments and evidence.

- **Ethos**: That's you proving that you are authoritative and trustworthy – share your expertise and experience to show why the audience should trust what you're telling them. What awards, prizes, or funding have you won? Where (and how long) have you taught? What is your expertise? How have you helped other students continue their study in related fields?

- **Pathos**: Play to the emotions by telling stories and anecdotes and sharing testimonials of how others felt. Lead with the emotional rewards of your product and how they'll make your client feel.

- **Logos**: Use logic and data to back up your point. Give statistics, case studies, and facts.

For example, I persuaded a client to purchase one of the company's premium packages because I provided them with an ROI analysis that supported the deal as well as a success story of a previous client which satisfied both their rational and emotional needs. Since sales is emotionally charged and based on trust, it's crucial to address both sides of the buyer's brain by proving that our deal is as beneficial as possible in the eyes of their logic and stakeholders and then sharing a compelling and 'human' story that taps into their emotional network.

3.5 Handling Objections

Handling objections effectively can turn a hesitant prospect into a committed client.

- **Expect the Counterargument**: There are a few common concerns to expect whenever you explain Impressionism and it's helpful to have some canned responses ready to go. Figure out the objections that you're likely to hear and prepare your answers to each one.

- **Listen First**: Listen carefully and always probe to make sure you understand the objection before trying to respond to it. Often the objection is really an expression of a need for more information or reassurance.

- **Rebuttal**: Acknowledge the objection and provide evidence or reassurance, showing empathy or understanding and framing your response in a positive way.

For example, a client explained: 'If the cost is a major challenge, it may take too long for us to implement it in our enterprise today.' My counter to that was: 'I can share our implementation plan with you. In addition, I am happy to connect you to one of our reference clients who will share their experience with implementation – this solution was installed with minimal disruption.' Another time, a client was concerned about the price: 'My CFO wouldn't sign off on it.' I showed her a customized ROI analysis showing she'd be paying back the investment in six months: 'That really makes a difference. Now I can sleep on it and I think we'll be fine next time we talk Rob.' Both times, I was able to address their hot button and help ease their concern – and both times, the prospect became a client.

3.6 Building Rapport

It's about gaining rapport with your client. You want to make them feel comfortable and valued.

- **Establish Common Ground**: What do the two of you have in common? Use an interest shared by both of you as a starting point in your conversation. Or both of you could have the same job.

- **Actually Care**: Ask about their goals and roadblocks and seek out what they need help with. Listen to understand.

- **Don't Be a Turd**: Authenticity builds trust and attraction. Be you, but get the tude right.

For example, 'I asked a client about marathon running and we found we were both enthusiasts. This made my communications with him go much smoother and we ended up closing a sale. Our mutual running background really helped us get along and we enjoyed working together.'

3.7 Time Management

Effective time management allows you to maximize productivity and maintain a healthy work-life balance.

- **Prioritize Tasks**: Work the sale. Focus on those high-value activities. What are your 'A' tasks – the things that actually draw income into your business? Do them first.

- **Work Your Tools**: Use calendars, task managers, and CRM tools to stay on top of your workflow. Trello, Asana, and Salesforce are all worth checking out.

- **Set Boundaries**: Your employer has the right to expect you to work when you're paid to work. But that is all. Your employer does not have the right to burn you out by imposing a vigorous work schedule and never giving you time to refuel. This is simply a line you do not want to cross.

For example, when I blocked times to prospect for new business, to return client calls, and to follow up with prospects, I was closing more business without hiring any new people, without keeping my inbox in the 'zillions' and without working more than 40 hours a week.

3.8 Continuous Learning

The sales landscape is constantly evolving and continuous learning is key to staying ahead.

- **Keep Up On Trends, Tools, and Techniques**: Subscribe to industry newsletters and blogs, listen to podcasts, and so on.

- **Seek Feedback**: Get regular feedback from live clients and peers on how you can do better. Negative feedback, when handled right, can be a great source of learning.

- **Training**: Why not invest in yourself? Participate in workshops, webinars, and training programs that the organization offers – not only to keep abreast of changing trends but also to further develop your skillset.

For example, I attend sales training seminars every three months and read the newest books on how to be a great salesperson. Because of this learning, I have stayed current with the newest closing techniques and I can be more successful at my job. I was recently taught about the new version of CRM that your company uses and have now been able to use all the newest features and make my sales process more efficient.

3.9 Storytelling in Sales

Storytelling is a powerful tool to make your pitch more engaging and relatable.

- **Structure**: A clear beginning, middle, and end. If a story is structured – it has a clear beginning, middle, and end – then it is less likely to be forgotten.

- **Relevance**: Make sure that the story is relevant to the client's situation and that you're using stories that reflect the client's own needs and problems.

- **Be Personal and Emotional**: Put heart and feeling into it (so clients remember the story). When storytelling is full of feeling, then clients will feel it too.

For example, I once told a story of a mom-and-pop owner who had turned their business around using our service. The story helped a prospect who was facing that exact challenge close his deal. He saw himself in the story and the possible ending.

3.10 Questioning Techniques

Asking the right questions can uncover valuable insights and steer the conversation.

- **Open-Ended Questions**: Encourage fine-grained answers and high-quality dialogue: 'You said last week you couldn't seem to stick to your routine, could you tell me more about how that challenges you?'

- **Question-Asking**: Get to the bottom of what a client is trying to tell you but does not know how to articulate. Great questions to ask would be: 'What do you mean by that?' or 'Can you elaborate on that? I'm not quite getting it.'

- **Leading Questions**: Ask low-risk questions that can gently move someone towards discovering or believing in the benefits of your product. Questions such as 'How would it feel to have a way to (manage this problem) completely?' help the client envision success.

For example, 'What are the challenges with your current solution?' This brought out pain points that our product could alleviate and provided a sharper focus for the sale. It triggered conversation about specific pain points that I could loop back to features of our solution.

3.11 Closing Techniques

Closing techniques are strategies used to seal the deal effectively.

- **Assumptive Close**: Act like the prospect is sold: 'When would you like to start the implementation process?'

- **Agreement Close**: Have the prospect reiterate the purchasing benefits: 'I agree _____ comes in three engaging modules and will elevate your conversion rate to new heights.'

- **Speed Up**: Eg 'This offer is available this month only.'

- **Summary-Close**: Recap the benefits to reinforce the value proposition. Recapping the high points and benefits refreshes the client's reasons for being interested.

For example, this assumptive close with a client: 'When would you like to start the implementation process?' This simple statement served as a nudge to dispatch the decision from the 'thinking' part to the 'doing' part by shifting the conversation from consideration to action resulting in a successful close. Of course, he appreciated the confidence and clarity of my position which made the decision much easier.

3.12 Developing Emotional Intelligence

Emotional intelligence (EQ) is important in self-awareness and management of our own feelings as well as that of others.

- **Self-Understanding**: Identify and monitor your feelings and see how you project them into your interactions. Awareness of your emotional triggers helps you to stay cool and collected.

- **Empathy**: Try to understand and share your clients' feelings and emotions with them. By being empathetic, you can build a rapport with the clients and help them resolve their worries.

- **Social Skills**: Deal effectively with the complexities of human relationships and build a wide and deep network of friends and allies. Having good social skills equips you to smooth out relationship frictions and talk through points of disagreement.

For instance, a client was so stressed over the phone. I really took my time, respected the person behind that call, and calmed him down with my patience and empathy. That helped complete the deal. He trusted me. He knew I had possibly lived through the same situation too.

Conclusion

Mastering these essential skills for selling will put you on the path towards becoming a remote closer of high-ticket deals. These skills, from active listening to effective communication, negotiation, persuasion, and more, are foundational to your success. With continuous learning and improvement, you can excel in the high-ticket remote closing landscape.

Chapter 4: Mastering Digital Tools

"Technology is best when it brings people together." - Matt Mullenweg

4.1 CRM Software Overview

The centrepiece of any remote-closing operation is the CRM (Customer Relationship Management) software you use to manage client interactions, track leads and guide prospective clients through the sales journey.

- **What It Is:** CRM software is a database tool that lets you track and manage all of your contacts with existing and prospective customers – your 'client relationship management' software. Think: Rolodex times 10.

- **Why It Matters:** It centralises all your client information in one place, for managing relationships and following up on leads, as well as data crunching – get to know your clients, keep them close to you and boil it down to relevant insights to improve your service, for instance. Keep all the interactions and information about a client in sight – the sales history and future steps are now close at hand.

- **Popular CRMs:** Salesforce, HubSpot and Zoho CRM come up top in most searches. There are strengths with each of these, such as Salesforce has a great customisation feature, HubSpot is easy to use, and Zoho is budget-friendly, while also offering a lot of bells and whistles.

For example, I used HubSpot to automate follow-up emails, track client's interactions, and generate reports about my activity in the sales process, which increased my productivity and closing rates. For instance, I would automate workflows to send customised follow-ups to a client, based on how they had engaged with me, decreasing the need for manual outreach.

4.2 Video Conferencing Tools

Remote closers need to use video conferencing tools so that they can meet their clients face to face, whatever part of the world they might be.

What It Is: A type of software that allows people to make video calls or hold internet meetings. Facilities typically include the ability to share your desktop, record your meetings, and impose a virtual backdrop.

Why it Matters: It enables you to communicate and collaborate in the same moment, enhance relationships with clients, and give more compelling presentations. It is easier to establish trust and rapport when clients can see you in real time, rather than via email or on the phone.

It goes without saying that Zoom, Microsoft Teams and Google Meet are the predominant tools. Everyone knows Zoom – it's most famous for being the de facto remote working platform, as it's easy to use and relatively stable when compared with its competitors.

Microsoft Teams is also popular, as it works well with the rest of the Microsoft Office suite. If only all its products were this easy to use!

Example: I recently used Zoom to walk a client, in a time zone thousands of miles away, through an itemised product demonstration. Thanks to the platform's screen-sharing capability, I could click through features, explain how things work in real time, and gauge their micro-expressions, et al – all in the context of present 'me' and 'you' experience. In layman's terms, I could read their body language and hop right into questions and tweaks, and fit more into one session.

4.3 Email Management Systems

If you are in a remote sales role, email is likely one of your primary communication methods. That even for a busy person, how you deal with email has a considerable impact on your ability to get things done.

- **What It Is:** Tools that help you organize, automate, and manage your email communications.

- **Why It Matters:** Your inbox stays organised, however many clients you might have; follow-ups get automated so you don't have to remember each and every one; and email opens and responses can be tracked so you know who has read what. Good email management helps you keep on top of your communications and respond promptly to enquiries from clients.

- **Most Popular Systems:** Gmail with Boomerang, Outlook, Mailchimp. Boomerang for Gmail lets you compose emails in advance and schedule sending, specifying reminders if a person you wrote doesn't reply, which is super helpful for keeping on top of client communications.

For example, I used Boomerang to schedule follow-up emails to clients who hadn't responded to my initial email in a week. This way, there would be no in-between time when a lead would fall through the cracks. I also scheduled reminders for when to follow up to keep on track and stay consistent with my prospective clients. This led to more closed deals.

4.4 Messaging Apps and Chatbots

Messaging apps and chatbots provide instant communication channels for quick responses and automated interactions.

- **What It Is:** Platforms that facilitate real-time messaging and automated chat responses.

- **Why it's important:** your clients' issues and inquiries can be resolved and your sales process expedited by getting instant answers to their questions. A chatbot will be able to handle all the less complex issues, so you can spend more time on the more involved sales interactions. On your website, chatbots are critical for gaining leads and helping customers with their queries 247.

Popular Apps

- Slack– great for internal team communication

- WhatsApp– allows you to send messages to your clients

- Intercom– contains interactive chatbots to interact with your clients while on your website.

For example, I used Intercom's chatbot to reply to first-time enquiries on my website. When there were common questions, the chatbot gave responses and gathered lead information that I would later follow-up. With Intercom, no potential client went through the waiting period as their questions were answered instantly. This feature is more pleasing to potential consumers, capturing more leads.

4.5 Social Media Platforms

Social media is a powerful tool for lead generation and client engagement.

- **Creation:** Sites where users can create and post original content, such as fan fiction or artworks. • Social: Sites where users can upload, share or otherwise participate in social networks, such as Facebook and Instagram.

- **Why It Matters:** You can use these to showcase your expertise, nurture relationships with prospects, and generate leads through content marketing. You can cast the widest net possible on social media, and interact with your audience more casually (and humanly).

- **Social:** LinkedIn, Facebook and Twitter. LinkedIn is by far the best social channel for B2B sales or networking.

Example: After posting a few articles providing inside info on how I go about my job, responding to and commenting on industry-related posts, and sharing my views, I started getting connected to meaningful relationships with potential clients, some of whom yielded multi-thousand-dollar sales. Posting articles, answering questions, and keeping timelines updated helped to facilitate my standing out as an authority in my niche.

_____

4.6 Analytics and Reporting Tools

Performance is measured by the analytics and reporting tools that give you insights into your sales activity.

- **What It Is:** Software that allows you to gather, analyse, and display data so you can make better choices.

- **What It Does:** It lets you see whether you can make more sales if you adjust your tactics. You will know what works, what doesn't work, and where improvements can be made in your sales approach.

- **Google Analytics, Tableau, Salesforce Analytics:** These are popular tools for tracking metadata on the web. You could use them to create a dashboard that visually shows where users are coming from and what they're doing on your website, helping you understand which marketing efforts are generating leads.

For Instance via Google Analytics, I tracked which blog posts were generating the most inbound website traffic for me, so I could then strive to write more similar content to appeal to those readers and generate still more leads. With a sense of my traffic source, I could adjust my marketing efforts accordingly to focus on driving more leads.

4.7 Automation Tools

Automation tools streamline repetitive tasks, saving you time and ensuring consistency.

• **What It Is:** Multipurpose algorithms for automating repetitive tasks such as chasing up emails, entering data, or posting to social media.

Why this matters: it helps you work smarter, avoiding human frailties, and leaving more time to be a strategic operator. Automating ensures an activity will actually happen (you're more likely to act on scheduling) and do so in a timely, consistent manner.

• **Common Tools:** Zapier, HubSpot, Mailchimp. A PM tool to link up various apps and manage workflows between them.

Eg: Using Zapier, I setup things so that, as each new lead comes in from a form on the site, they are automatically added to my CRM and emailed a simple welcome note. No manual intervention is required if I want my 'funnel' to operate invisibly, while helping me spend more time on what will truly seal the deal – person-to-person interaction. By automating these early stages, ie those that require little follow-up, I can rather elevate the time I spend on the parts of the equation that do.

_____

4.8 Integrating Tools for Efficiency

Integrating various tools can enhance your workflow and improve efficiency.

- **What It Is:** Combining different software tools to work seamlessly together.

- **So What:** users don't have to worry about ending one app and opening another; what was being done can continue. One big value of integrated tools is that it reduces the number of times the user is concerned with switching from one task to another and so eliminates the context switching – the worry about what was just being done so that it can continue. Integrated tools make work go better and make data easier to work on.

- **How to Do It:** Use integration platforms such as Zapier or native integrations provided by the software. Many CRMs come with their native integrations with email systems, social media and analytics tools.

For example, to integrate my customer relationship management (CRM) with my email management system and calendar, I can track emails, schedule follow ups and appointments, and automate administration, thereby increasing my sales activity and saving time. Integration of these systems allowed me to better manage my time and ease some of my administrative burdens to make my sales process more efficient.

_____

4.9 Choosing the Right Tools

Choosing the right tools depends on your specific needs and preferences.

- **What Are Your Needs?** Make a list of what you absolutely need your system to perform (e.g., do you want it to track leads; is there a need to automate emails; do you need analytics?). Think about your sales workflow and what tasks are most crucial to your process and the tools that could help manage or automate them.

- **Choose one or more:** Compare features, usability and cost of different available tools. Find parsers that provide the functionality at a price worth paying.

- **Test Before Buying:** With many tools offering free trials, it's easy to see how they might work for you. Testing the tools in a real workflow will help you determine if they have the features you need or how you would incorporate them if they checked all your boxes.

For instance: Before settling on HubSpot, I tested four or five CRMs to find which had the best feature-functionality-price tradeoff. Each one offered a free trial period, so I dug in and tried out each tool for several of my smaller clients – seeing how each one would work for 'the job'. Testing my options helped me find a tool that would truly support my sales outbound efforts.

4.10 Training on Digital Tools

Proper training on digital tools is essential to maximize their effectiveness.

• **REASON:** Training lets you and your staff use the tools at their best, so you don't buy to underuse or waste their benefits. • ROI: Without the right training for users and maintenance staff in new tools, they'll fail to be properly used or miss vital functions and upgrades.

• **Training:** Enjoy the online tutorials, webinars and training courses of your software provider. Most tools come with ample learning resources that enable you to become a good user quickly.

• **Training:** Prioritise updating your skills so you can stay abreast of new features and best practices. You don't want to be behind the times with your tools.

Example: I took several webinars with HubSpot's team to better understand its features so that I could use its CRM functionalities in the best way possible. Thanks to HubSpot's training, I learnt how to maximise the use of the tool, for example with automated workflow and advanced reporting features, and this allowed me to increase my productivity. Furthermore, every session I attended was an opportunity for me to be informed about new features and updates – this made sure I used the tool in the most effective way.

4.11 Security and Privacy

Ensuring the security and privacy of your data and client information is critical.

• **Why:** Allowing users to encrypt their data on your site is a way to demonstrate your respect for their privacy, and also helps you stay compliant with the GDPR, a European privacy law. Data security scandals can significantly harm your brand; they can also trigger legal penalties.

Best Practices: Strong unique passwords, two-factor authentication, software updates, team training Sounds basic, but if you do all these things, you will reduce your odds of a breach by something more than half.

• **Use Strong Tools:** Use tools developed by well-established companies, with strong track records of security. Good security indicators are third-party certifications and compliance standards, such as FISMA, or federal information security management act in the US; ISO/IEC 27001 certification, an international standard outlining best practices to manage information security; or HIPAA, a US federal privacy law relating to the handling of personal data. These certifications can be verified, ensuring expertise. Specific requirements include data encryption from user to server end, secure and encrypted servers, and audits of products for security vulnerabilities.

Example: I use an application called LastPass to organise and safely store all my passwords, while ensuring that all my accounts have strong, unique passwords. I also use two-factor authentication on all of my accounts. I share best practices with my team, and regularly perform security audits.

4.12 Keeping Up with Technology Trends

Staying updated with technology trends ensures you remain competitive and efficient.

- Why It Matters:There is new technology available everyday.If we keep up to date with things and follow new trends,this can help our workflow become more effective.By using new technolgy before our competitors we can have a significant advantage.

- How to stay on top: Keep up with industry news, listen to webinars, join professional associations and networks, join groups or seek out peers in social media. Don't forget to subscribe to tech newsletters and go to industry conferences every once in a while.

- Use New Tools: Be willing to try out and use new tools that help you become more productive. Always monitor the tools you've currently adopted and be willing to switch tools if something better comes along.

Example: I always read industry newsletters, and make an effort to attend tech conferences in order to be knowledgeable about what's happening, and to pick up on new tools for the future. This has resulted in me being able to enhance my working life before most – taking the plunge and adopting new technologies early, such as AI-powered analytics tools which have revolutionised my decision-making. These tools have enabled me to organise how I spend my time and be far more effective overall.

Conclusion

And learning to use the technology that helps you figure out, achieve, and 'close' on high-ticket transactions remotely is particularly crucial. In this world, your toolset – CRM software, video conferencing, automation, analytics – can make or break your workflow, and your productivity. Know where to buy the tools that make you most efficient, know how to thread them together, and stay at the front of the tool tsunami. These are the keys to conquering the space.

Next, we'll discuss the sales process and look at each step individually to make sure you have the focus and tactics required to close the sale. Over, and out.

Chapter 5: The Sales Process

"Every sale has five basic obstacles: no need, no money, no hurry, no desire, no trust." - Zig Ziglar

5.1 Lead Generation

Lead generation is the initial part of the sales process when you find people who might potentially need your product or service.

- **What It Is:** The process of attracting and converting strangers into prospects.

- **Why It Matters:** If you don't have leads, you don't have potential customers to sell anything to. It's your blood flow.

- **Techniques:** Content marketing, social media marketing, email campaigns, SEO, paid advertising, and networking.

Example: When I deliver talks virtually to sales teams, I am marketing myself as a remote closer. In between the talks, I post updates to discuss the sales-enablement industry, as well as sharing insights from other thought leaders from the sales-enablement community. This attracts my target market of business professionals, and they end up contacting me, which leads to consultations. By posting regular content – including articles around key sales trends, features, and case studies that feature my clients' successes – my craft allows a consistent stream of qualified leads who are interested in working with me. One of my articles on the latest advances in sales automation tools triggered multiple inquiries from businesses looking to streamline their sales process.

5.2 Initial Contact and Qualification

With those leads in hand, get in touch and qualify those prospects to ensure they're suitable for your product.

- **What It Is:** Contacting leads to understand if they will move to the opportunity stage.

- **Why It Matters:** Qualification helps you focus on leads that are most likely to convert, saving you time and money.

- **Techniques:** Email outreach, cold calling, social media messaging, and lead scoring based on criteria that can be defined in advance.

For example, I will ask the lead in the first call certain qualifying questions about their needs, budget, and decision-making process – such as: 'What are your challenges?'; 'What budget have you allocated?' Firstly, these questions help me fully understand if the lead is going to be a good fit or not, and whether I should adapt my offering to their situation or suggest a solution found at a different vendor. Secondly, this kind of qualification will show that the lead's budget is outside our minimum package – and that's good for both of us because it's a category of lead that we can't serve, and it therefore saves us time and helps us drill down on leads that are more viable.

5.3 Building Relationships

If you want to build a two-sided relationship with your targets, you need to know what they want and also earn their trust.

- **What It Is:** Cultivating a bond to your prospects based upon trust and honour.

- **Why It Matters:** Close relationships improve your chances of making a sale and instil trust in clients you hope to have for a long time.

- **Techniques:** Active listening, regular follow-ups, personalized communication, and providing value through insights and advice.

For instance: 'Every three weeks, make a point of sending the prospect whatever you read on their specific industry. If they are doing it wrong, send them a specific guide on what they need to fix. Be the reference. Do it enough times, and they'll reward you when it's time to buy'. Example: Had a prospect struggling on lead generation. I sent him a killer detailed guide on ultimate advanced lead generation. Not only did he improve his efforts, the expert status also led to a sale.

5.4 Presenting Your Offer

The next step is to pitch your offer: explaining how your product or service can solve the prospect's problem or fulfil their need.

- **What It Is:** Explaining the value of your product/service and its features to your prospect.

- **Why It Matters:** A strong reasons section can make a powerful case for why the prospect should buy from you.

- **Techniques:** Tailored presentations, product demos, case studies, and ROI analysis.

Example: I customize every pitch I do to the prospect's pain points. If a prospect has a problem with team productivity, I'll highlight features of our solution that help to streamline workflows and improve collaboration. If I can do a live demo that will show them how it benefits them, I will. I did one demo to a tech company where I mentioned that we could reduce their project turnaround time by 30 per cent, which means more projects being done in the same time. Putting it as a clear, tangible benefit made the whole offer more enticing.

5.5 Handling Objections

Handling objections effectively can turn a hesitant prospect into a committed client.

- **What It Is:** The act of responding to and resolving responses or objections from prospects.

- **Why It Matters:** Successfully handling objections can remove barriers to closing the deal.

- **Techniques:** Pre-empting common counter-arguments, reflecting back what you've heard's true cause, and offering proof or reassurance.

For example, one prospect complained about how long it would take to get my product implemented. I gave her a detailed implementation plan and then told her how few of my current customers experienced any downtime in implementing: "Everyone was happy with Vanessa's plan and happy with the fact that when it was done, the store worked better than before, and no one even noticed the change." Another time, a client was concerned about the price: 'My CFO wouldn't sign off on it.' I showed her a customized ROI analysis showing she'd be paying back the investment in six months: 'That really makes a difference. Now I can sleep on it, and I think we'll be fine next time we talk, Rob.' Both times I was able to address their hot button and help ease their concern – and both times the prospect became a client.

5.6 Closing the Deal

Getting the prospect to sign on the dotted line is the final step, often referred to as closing the deal.

- **What It Is:** Closing and getting the promise from the prospect.

- **Why It Matters:** Closing is a result of all your pre-work and puts money into your pocket.

- **Techniques:** Assumptive close, urgency close, summary close, and trial close.

For example, I closed a sale with the assumptive close: a client had called me to find apartments, and I said to him, 'When do you want to get started on the implementation process?' By nudging the client along from the deliberation stage to the implementation stage, I ensured the close. Changing the question's tone from 'When would you like to get started on the implementation process?' to 'Would you like to get started on the implementation process?' made all the difference to the client. He answered: 'Yeah.' On another deal, I used the trial close. I asked a client who was wavering from his commitment to purchase a car: 'If we can solve your problem 'X', will you be ready to move forward?' The trial close worked because it addressed the last-minute objection.

5.7 Follow-Up Strategies

Without a follow-up, the momentum is lost, and the opportunity is gone.

- **What It Is:** All the contact and touching base steps between when you first reach out to a prospect and when you present your programme.

- **Why It Matters:** Follow-up questions are crucial to turning a no into a yes. Tracking objections helps you identify and eliminate roadblocks.

- **Techniques:** Scheduled follow-up emails, phone calls, and personalized messages.

For example, my CRM triggers reminders to set up a follow-up, and based on the context, I have email-bots to send out a sequence of messages to walk the prospect through different actions. Right after a first meeting, I send a follow-up email summarizing the conversation and outlining next steps with clear instructions so that my prospect knows what to expect from me. Example: after a demo, I send a follow-up email with some resources and suggest a timeline for next steps. I've found that this method of structured follow-up has helped me convert not-so-sure prospects.

5.8 Post-Sale Relationship Management

Maintaining relationships after the sale is crucial for client satisfaction and long-term success.

- **What It Is:** Relationship management or caretaking with people who have already bought from you.

- **Why It Matters:** Post-sale engagement leads to repeat business, referrals, and positive reviews.

- **Techniques:** Regular check-ins, providing ongoing support, and offering additional value through resources and updates.

Model: Routinely after a deal has closed, I check in to see how the person liked the purchase and to help out in any way I could. By providing them with ongoing support and resources, I was able to keep clients very happy in their purchases, and this led to many referrals. For instance, I had a client of mine who initially I thought was very pleased with their purchase. Later on, they started having issues during the implementation phase. By routinely checking they were happy and checking on the projects' progress and timeline, I was able to help with the challenges they faced. This help, along with additional training, ensured they were able to stay on track and adopt the solution successfully. We have been working together for years now.

5.9 Sales Funnel Stages

If you know what stage your prospects are in, this will help you manage that sales funnel for peak efficiency with CRM.

- **What It Is:** The sequence of stages a prospect goes through on its way to a final purchase.

- **Why It Matters:** Understanding what happens at each funnel step will let you apply the right set of strategies for each 'conversion' from one stage to the next to get a prospect closer to a sale.

- **Stages:** Awareness, Interest, Consideration, Intent, Evaluation, Purchase.

For example, I break down my sales process into what version of the funnel my prospect is in and develop tactics specific to each. If the prospect is in the consideration stage, I need to focus on giving them details and case studies. At the evaluation stage, I need to answer the distinction and ROI questions. The interest stage might involve sending some educational content so I can become a source of information, but I want to make sure there are no education gaps. At the intent stage, I want to offer a personalized demo to close out remaining objections or to address nuances only their deal would cover.

5.10 Converting Leads to Customers

Moving leads to customers means following them through the sales funnel and their requirements from each stage.

- **What It Is:** The process of turning interested prospects into paying customers.

- **Why It Matters:** Effective conversion strategies increase your closing rate and revenue.

- **Techniques:** Personalized communication, timely follow-ups, and value-driven presentations.

Example: I have converted a number of leads who at a surface level seemed reluctant. How I presented our value proposition and then followed up depended on the lead adapting to their needs and interests. I excelled and closed sales by, for example, customizing my initial pitch to address a lead's pain points and demonstrate how we solve specific issues. Of course, I also asked about their pains and needs. A prospect told me that the fear of not being able to scale was an important concern for him and his company. I immediately researched one of our clients in his industry and described how we scaled up for them. I shared details such as the exact platform we used and highlighted our most recent performance numbers, effectively closing the sale.

5.11 Measuring Sales Performance

Measuring sales performance helps you understand what's working and where you need to improve.

- **What It Is:** The process of tracking and analyzing key sales metrics.

- **Why It Matters:** Performance measurement is about learning. The results can tell you what to tinker with to improve your outcome.

- **Metrics:** Conversion rate, average deal size, sales cycle length, and lead-to-customer ratio.

Model answer: I pay attention to my sales figures constantly to see what's changing and where. I analyzed the conversion rates, the effect of different marketing techniques, and decided to tweak my process to improve my closing rate. Through reorganizing my time to have more initial calls and subsequently more follow-ups where I was able to close 20 per cent of sales within 24 hours of the first call, I figured out the best thing for me. For example, my data showed that if I call a lead up within the first day of making contact, I'm twice more likely to convert, and so I tried to have more initial calls subsequently making more follow-ups where I managed to close 20 per cent of my sales through closing within 24 hours of a phone call.

5.12 Continuous Improvement

Continuous improvement involves regularly refining your sales process based on feedback and performance data.

- **What It Is:** The ongoing process of evaluating and enhancing your sales strategies.

- **Why It Matters:** If you're not moving forward, you're losing ground. If you're not finding ways to constantly and immediately improve, you're losing clients.

- **Techniques:** Gathering feedback, analyzing performance data, and implementing new strategies.

Example: I elicit feedback on my work from clients after every sale and then apply it to help improve my tactics. In one case, feedback on the clarity of my presentations prompted me to simplify my slides and focus on key benefits to clarify my sales pitch and enable them to better understand my advice. I also attend sales training courses and workshops as part of my professional development to continue learning about the latest techniques and best practices so that my toolkit and tactics don't go stale.

Conclusion

There are multiple stages to this, each with a specific need that requires a specific skill to entice the prospect to the next step in the funnel. Regardless of the size of your business, if you're selling anything as a big ticket, then a part of the process will be trying to convert your prospects to clients. But before you can sell something, you first have to generate leads to attract prospects. If you want to take your high-ticket remote close to the next level, you need to examine each stage and refine your techniques as you take your business to a new level.

Now let's talk about high-ticket sales… how to incorporate these tips and how to scale. Let's get busy!

Chapter 6: High-Ticket Sales Techniques

"Selling is not about selling anymore, but about building trust and educating." - Siva Devaki

6.1 Value-Based Selling

Value-based selling focuses on the benefits and value your product or service brings to the customer rather than the features.

- **What It Is:** A sales technique that emphasizes the value your solution provides to the customer.

- **Why It Matters:** Customers are more likely to buy if they see a clear benefit or ROI.

- **Techniques:** Identify the customer's pain points, highlight how your solution addresses these issues, and provide examples of tangible benefits.

Example: During a pitch, instead of listing all the features of my software, I focus on how it can save the client time and increase their productivity. I share case studies showing how previous clients have seen a 30% reduction in project completion time, which translates to significant cost savings and higher revenue.

6.2 Solution Selling

Solution selling involves understanding the customer's needs and providing a tailored solution that addresses those needs.

- **What It Is:** A method that focuses on selling solutions to problems rather than products.

- **Why It Matters:** This approach positions you as a consultant rather than a salesperson, building trust and credibility.

- **Techniques:** Conduct thorough needs analysis, customize your proposal, and show how your solution specifically addresses the client's challenges.

Example: For a client struggling with managing remote teams, I tailored my proposal to show how our project management tool offers real-time collaboration features, task tracking, and performance analytics. This approach demonstrated that I understood their problem and had a solution designed to solve it.

6.3 SPIN Selling

SPIN Selling is a technique that uses four types of questions to understand the customer's needs: Situation, Problem, Implication, and Need-Payoff.

- **What It Is:** A questioning technique designed to uncover the buyer's needs and position your product as the solution.

- **Why It Matters:** It helps you understand the deeper motivations and pain points of your client.

- **Techniques:** Ask situation questions to understand the context, problem questions to identify issues, implication questions to highlight the consequences of not addressing the problem, and need-payoff questions to show the benefits of your solution.

Example: In a call with a potential client, I asked about their current project management process (Situation), the challenges they faced with remote teams (Problem), the impact of missed deadlines on their business (Implication), and how our tool could streamline their workflow and improve accountability (Need-Payoff). This structured approach helped the client see the value of our solution clearly.

6.4 Consultative Selling

Consultative selling involves acting as a trusted advisor to the client, offering expertise and guidance rather than just pushing a product.

- **What It Is:** A sales approach that prioritizes the client's needs and provides expert advice.

- **Why It Matters:** Builds strong relationships and positions you as a knowledgeable resource.

- **Techniques:** Conduct detailed discovery sessions, offer tailored recommendations, and provide ongoing support and follow-up.

Example: With a new client in the healthcare industry, I spent several sessions understanding their specific needs and regulatory requirements. I provided tailored recommendations on how our software could help them comply with industry standards and improve patient care. This consultative approach built trust and led to a long-term partnership.

6.5 Challenger Sales Model

The Challenger Sales Model involves taking control of the sales conversation and teaching the client something new about their business.

- **What It Is:** A sales approach that challenges the customer's assumptions and offers new insights.

- **Why It Matters:** Differentiates you from competitors and adds value to the client.

- **Techniques:** Teach the client something new, tailor your message to their specific needs, and take control of the sales process.

Example: In a meeting with a client in the retail sector, I presented data showing how their current inventory management system was costing them money. I then taught them how our system could reduce waste and improve profitability by providing real-time analytics and demand forecasting. This approach demonstrated my expertise and convinced them to switch to our solution.

6.6 Storytelling in Sales

Storytelling in sales uses narratives to make your pitch more engaging and relatable.

- **What It Is:** The use of stories to illustrate points and connect with the customer on an emotional level.

- **Why It Matters:** Stories are more memorable and can make complex concepts easier to understand.

- **Techniques:** Share success stories, use customer testimonials, and create scenarios that illustrate the benefits of your product.

Example: During a pitch, I shared a story about a client who was struggling with project delays and how our tool helped them streamline their processes, leading to a 40% increase in on-time delivery. This story resonated with the prospect and helped them visualize the benefits of our solution in their own context.

6.7 Leveraging Case Studies

Case studies provide concrete examples of how your product or service has helped other clients.

- **What It Is:** Detailed accounts of how your solution has benefited other customers.

- **Why It Matters:** Provides social proof and demonstrates the practical application of your product.

- **Techniques:** Highlight specific challenges, the solution provided, and the measurable results achieved.

Example: I shared a case study of a client in the financial services industry who used our software to reduce compliance errors by 50%. The case study detailed the challenges they faced, how our solution was implemented, and the significant improvements they experienced. This provided compelling evidence of our product's effectiveness.

6.8 Demonstrating ROI

Demonstrating ROI (Return on Investment) shows the financial benefits of your solution.

- **What It Is:** Calculating and presenting the financial returns a client can expect from using your product.

- **Why It Matters:** Helps justify the investment and makes a strong business case.

- **Techniques:** Provide ROI calculations, use real-world examples, and present cost-benefit analyses.

Example: For a prospect concerned about the cost of our software, I presented an ROI analysis showing how they could recoup their investment within six months through increased efficiency and reduced operational costs. I used specific data from similar clients to support my calculations, making the financial benefits clear and convincing.

6.9 Building Authority

Building authority involves establishing yourself as an expert in your field.

- **What It Is:** Positioning yourself as a knowledgeable and credible resource.

- **Why It Matters:** Clients are more likely to trust and buy from someone they see as an authority.

- **Techniques:** Share insights, publish content, speak at industry events, and engage in professional communities.

Example: I regularly publish articles on LinkedIn about sales strategies and remote closing techniques. By sharing valuable insights and participating in industry discussions, I've established myself as an authority in the field. This has led to speaking engagements and increased trust from prospects who view me as a credible expert.

6.10 Tailoring Proposals

Tailoring proposals means customizing your offer to meet the specific needs of each client.

- **What It Is:** Creating personalized proposals that address the unique requirements of each prospect.

- **Why It Matters:** Shows that you understand the client's needs and are committed to providing a solution that fits.

- **Techniques:** Include personalized recommendations, address specific pain points, and highlight relevant benefits.

Example: When preparing a proposal for a manufacturing client, I included details on how our software could integrate with their existing systems, reduce downtime, and improve production efficiency. By tailoring the proposal to their specific needs, I demonstrated our commitment to solving their problems and providing a customized solution.

6.11 Creating Persuasive Presentations

Creating persuasive presentations involves designing and delivering compelling presentations that capture the client's interest.

- **What It Is:** The process of crafting and presenting information in a way that persuades the client to take action.

- **Why It Matters:** A well-crafted presentation can make a powerful impact and increase the likelihood of closing the deal.

- **Techniques:** Use visual aids, tell a story, focus on benefits, and practice your delivery.

Example: For a presentation to a tech company, I used a combination of slides, demos, and customer testimonials to illustrate the benefits of our product. I structured the presentation to tell a story, starting with the client's challenges, presenting our solution, and highlighting the positive outcomes. This approach made the presentation engaging and persuasive.

6.12 Handling High-Pressure Situations

Handling high-pressure situations involves maintaining composure and confidence when dealing with challenging sales scenarios.

- **What It Is:** The ability to stay calm and effective under pressure.

- **Why It Matters:** High-pressure situations are common in sales, and how you handle them can make or break the deal.

- **Techniques:** Prepare thoroughly, practice stress-management techniques, and stay focused on the client's needs.

Example: During a high-stakes negotiation with a large corporate client, I encountered several objections and tough questions. By staying calm, listening carefully, and responding with well-prepared answers, I was able to address their concerns and demonstrate our value. This approach helped me close the deal despite the pressure.

Chapter 7: Building and Maintaining Client Relationships

"Customer relationships are like marriages. They require work and commitment to keep them fresh and exciting." - Shep Hyken

7.1 Establishing Initial Trust

Building trust with clients from the first interaction is crucial for long-term relationships.

- **What It Is:** The process of gaining the client's confidence and demonstrating reliability.

- **Why It Matters:** Trust is the foundation of all successful client relationships and influences their willingness to engage with you.

- **Techniques:** Be transparent, communicate clearly, and deliver on your promises.

Example: When I first connect with a new client, I make sure to be upfront about what we can achieve and any potential limitations. By setting clear expectations and consistently meeting them, I build a solid foundation of trust. For instance, I once told a client we couldn't meet a particular feature request in the initial phase but would work on it for future updates. This honesty helped establish a trustworthy relationship.

7.2 Personalized Communication

Personalized communication shows clients that you understand and care about their specific needs.

- **What It Is:** Tailoring your interactions and messages to each client's preferences and requirements.

- **Why It Matters:** Personalization makes clients feel valued and understood, fostering stronger relationships.

- **Techniques:** Use the client's name, reference past conversations, and tailor your recommendations to their needs.

Example: Instead of sending generic emails, I always include details that are specific to the client's business or previous discussions we've had. For instance, if a client mentioned a particular challenge in a past meeting, I address that challenge directly in my follow-up communication, providing relevant resources or solutions.

7.3 Consistent Follow-Up

Regular follow-ups show clients that you are attentive and committed to their success.

- **What It Is:** Maintaining regular contact with clients to keep the relationship active and address any ongoing needs.

- **Why It Matters:** Consistent follow-up demonstrates dedication and can help identify new opportunities or issues early.

- **Techniques:** Schedule regular check-ins, send updates on relevant topics, and be proactive in offering assistance.

Example: I set reminders to check in with clients every few weeks. During these follow-ups, I provide updates on their projects, share industry news that might interest them, and ask if there's anything else they need help with. This consistent engagement helps keep our relationship strong and ensures they feel supported.

7.4 Exceeding Expectations

Going above and beyond what is expected can significantly strengthen client relationships.

- **What It Is:** Delivering more than what the client anticipates in terms of service or results.

- **Why It Matters:** Exceeding expectations creates a memorable experience and builds loyalty.

- **Techniques:** Add value through additional resources, offer proactive solutions, and show appreciation for their business.

Example: For a client expecting a standard report, I included a detailed analysis with actionable insights and recommendations. This extra effort not only impressed the client but also demonstrated my commitment to their success. They appreciated the added value and continued to rely on my services for future projects.

7.5 Gathering and Implementing Feedback

Soliciting and acting on client feedback shows that you value their input and are committed to improvement.

- **What It Is:** The process of asking clients for their opinions and suggestions and using that information to enhance your services.

- **Why It Matters:** Feedback helps you understand client needs better and improve your offerings.

- **Techniques:** Conduct surveys, hold feedback sessions, and implement changes based on the feedback received.

Example: After completing a project, I always ask clients for their feedback on the process and the results. One client mentioned that they would prefer more frequent updates. I took this feedback to heart and adjusted my communication strategy for future projects, leading to higher client satisfaction.

7.6 Managing Client Expectations

Setting and managing client expectations is key to maintaining a positive relationship.

- **What It Is:** Clearly communicating what clients can expect in terms of deliverables, timelines, and outcomes.

- **Why It Matters:** Properly managed expectations prevent misunderstandings and ensure client satisfaction.

- **Techniques:** Set realistic goals, communicate timelines, and provide regular updates.

Example: Before starting a project, I discuss with the client what they can realistically expect in terms of results and timelines. By setting clear expectations upfront and providing regular progress updates, I ensure that there are no surprises and that the client remains satisfied throughout the process.

7.7 Long-Term Relationship Strategies

Focusing on long-term relationship strategies helps retain clients and encourages repeat business.

- **What It Is:** Strategies aimed at maintaining and enhancing client relationships over time.

- **Why It Matters:** Long-term clients are more valuable, providing ongoing revenue and referrals.

- **Techniques:** Offer ongoing support, regularly review and adjust services, and recognize milestones and achievements.

Example: I maintain long-term relationships by regularly reviewing the client's needs and adjusting our services accordingly. For example, a client who initially signed up for a basic service package later needed more advanced features. By proactively suggesting upgrades and additional services, I kept the relationship strong and continued to meet their evolving needs.

7.8 Turning Clients into Advocates

Satisfied clients can become advocates, promoting your services through word-of-mouth and referrals.

- **What It Is:** Encouraging satisfied clients to share their positive experiences and refer new business.

- **Why It Matters:** Client advocates can significantly boost your reputation and attract new clients.

- **Techniques:** Provide exceptional service, ask for testimonials, and create referral programs.

Example: After successfully completing a project, I asked the client for a testimonial and offered a referral incentive. The client provided a glowing review and referred two new businesses to me, both of which became clients. Their advocacy helped expand my network and build my reputation.

7.9 Celebrating Client Successes

Recognizing and celebrating your clients' successes helps build a positive and supportive relationship.

- **What It Is:** Acknowledging and celebrating significant achievements or milestones your clients reach.

- **Why It Matters:** Celebrating successes shows that you are invested in their growth and builds goodwill.

- **Techniques:** Send congratulatory messages, feature their success stories, and offer small tokens of appreciation.

Example: When a client achieved a major business milestone, I sent a congratulatory email and featured their success story in my newsletter. This recognition made the client feel valued and appreciated, strengthening our relationship and encouraging ongoing collaboration.

7.10 Addressing Client Concerns Proactively

Proactively addressing client concerns helps prevent issues from escalating and shows that you are attentive to their needs.

- **What It Is:** Identifying and addressing potential issues before they become major problems.

- **Why It Matters:** Proactive problem-solving builds trust and demonstrates commitment to client satisfaction.

- **Techniques:** Monitor client interactions, regularly check in, and address concerns promptly.

Example: I noticed a client's engagement metrics were declining, so I reached out to discuss potential issues and offer solutions. By addressing the concern proactively, I prevented the problem from escalating and provided valuable support that improved the client's satisfaction.

7.11 Building a Community

Creating a community around your brand helps clients feel connected and engaged.

- **What It Is:** Building a network of clients who interact with each other and your brand.

- **Why It Matters:** A strong community fosters loyalty, encourages referrals, and provides valuable feedback.

- **Techniques:** Host events, create online forums, and encourage client interactions.

Example: I created an online forum where clients could share their experiences, ask questions, and provide feedback. This community became a valuable resource for clients to connect and learn from each other, enhancing their overall experience and loyalty to my brand.

7.12 Leveraging Client Referrals

Client referrals are a powerful way to grow your business through word-of-mouth marketing.

- **What It Is:** Encouraging existing clients to refer new clients to your business.

- **Why It Matters:** Referrals are a cost-effective way to acquire new clients and build trust quickly.

- **Techniques:** Offer referral incentives, make it easy for clients to refer others, and show appreciation for referrals.

Example: I implemented a referral program that offered clients a discount on their next service for each new client they referred. This program incentivized referrals and helped grow my client base significantly. One client referred three new businesses in just a few months, leading to substantial growth and increased revenue.

Chapter 8: Advanced Closing Strategies

"The close of a sale is just the beginning of a relationship." - B.J. Bueno

8.1 The Assumptive Close

The Assumptive Close is all about acting as if the client has already decided to purchase, which nudges them towards a positive decision.

- What It Is: This technique assumes the sale is already made.

- Why It Matters: It helps create a sense of inevitability, prompting the client to commit.

- Techniques: Use phrases like "When you start using our product…" or "You will see these benefits…".

Example: In a conversation with a prospect, I said, "When you start using our software, you'll notice an immediate improvement in your team's productivity." This assumptive language helped the prospect envision the benefits and led to a quicker close.

The Assumptive Close is all about acting as if the client has already decided to purchase, which nudges them towards a positive decision.

- **What It Is:** This technique assumes the sale is already made.

- **Why It Matters:** It helps create a sense of inevitability, prompting the client to commit.

- **Techniques:** Use phrases like "When you start using our product..." or "You will see these benefits...".

Example: In a conversation with a prospect, I said, "When you start using our software, you'll notice an immediate improvement in your team's productivity." This assumptive language helped the prospect envision the benefits and led to a quicker close.

8.2 The Urgency Close

The Urgency Close leverages time-sensitive offers to encourage the client to make a decision quickly.

- **What It Is:** A technique that creates a sense of urgency to prompt immediate action.
- **Why It Matters:** It motivates clients to act quickly to take advantage of a limited-time offer.
- **Techniques:** Highlight limited availability, special pricing, or upcoming deadlines.

Example: I offered a prospect a discount that was only valid for the next 48 hours. By emphasizing the time-sensitive nature of the offer, I encouraged them to make a decision quickly, resulting in a successful close.

8.3 The Takeaway Close

The Takeaway Close involves suggesting that the client may miss out on the offer, creating a fear of loss.

- **What It Is:** A technique that uses the possibility of withdrawal to push the client towards a decision.
- **Why It Matters:** People are often motivated by the fear of losing out on an opportunity.
- **Techniques:** Indicate that the offer is being reconsidered or that it might not be available later.

Example: When a prospect was hesitant, I said, "I understand if you're not ready now, but we might not have this special package available later." This statement created a sense of urgency and helped the prospect decide to move forward with the purchase.

8.4 The Alternative Close

The Alternative Close offers the client a choice between two options, both of which lead to a sale.

- **What It Is:** A closing technique that gives the client a choice between two positive outcomes.

- **Why It Matters:** It makes the decision-making process easier and leads to a commitment.

- **Techniques:** Present two options and ask the client to choose between them.

Example: I asked a client, "Would you prefer the standard package with monthly support or the premium package with 24/7 support?" By framing the options as a choice rather than a yes/no decision, I guided the client towards making a purchase.

8.5 The Summary Close

The Summary Close involves summarizing the key benefits and features of your product to reinforce the client's decision.

- **What It Is:** A technique that reviews the main points of your offer to remind the client of its value.

- **Why It Matters:** It reinforces the benefits and helps the client feel confident in their decision.

- **Techniques:** Recap the benefits, features, and any agreed terms before asking for the commitment.

Example: Before closing a deal, I summarized the key benefits of our software, including increased productivity, cost savings, and enhanced team collaboration. This recap reassured the client of their decision and led to a successful close.

8.6 The Scarcity Close

The Scarcity Close leverages the limited availability of your offer to prompt immediate action.

- **What It Is:** A closing technique that emphasizes the limited nature of the offer.

- **Why It Matters:** Scarcity can create a sense of urgency and motivate the client to act quickly.

- **Techniques:** Highlight limited stock, exclusive offers, or time-sensitive promotions.

Example: I informed a client that we only had a few spots left for our premium service package. This scarcity created urgency and led the client to commit to the purchase before the opportunity was gone.

8.7 The Direct Close

The Direct Close involves straightforwardly asking the client for the sale.

- **What It Is:** A technique that involves directly asking for the client's commitment.

- **Why It Matters:** It eliminates ambiguity and brings the conversation to a clear conclusion.

- **Techniques:** Use direct language such as "Are you ready to move forward?" or "Can we go ahead with the order?"

Example: After presenting my proposal, I asked the client directly, "Are you ready to move forward with this plan?" This clear and direct approach helped the client make a quick decision, resulting in a successful close.

8.8 Adapting Closing Techniques

Adapting your closing techniques to fit the client's needs and the sales context is crucial for success.

- **What It Is:** The practice of tailoring your closing strategy to the specific situation and client.

- **Why It Matters:** Different clients and situations may require different approaches for effective closing.

- **Techniques:** Assess the client's personality, preferences, and the context of the sale to choose the most appropriate closing technique.

Example: For a cautious client, I used a more consultative approach, providing detailed information and addressing all their concerns before using the summary close. For a decisive client, I opted for the direct close to quickly secure the sale.

8.9 The Value Close

The Value Close focuses on reinforcing the value and benefits of your product or service.

- **What It Is:** A closing technique that emphasizes the value your solution brings to the client.

- **Why It Matters:** Highlighting value helps justify the investment and reassures the client of their decision.

- **Techniques:** Recap the key benefits, share success stories, and quantify the value in terms of ROI.

Example: I reinforced the value of our software by sharing a case study of a client who saw a 40% increase in productivity and significant cost savings. This emphasis on value helped the prospect see the tangible benefits and led to a successful close.

8.10 The Time-Limited Offer Close

The Time-Limited Offer Close creates a sense of urgency by making the offer available for a limited time.

- **What It Is:** A technique that uses a deadline to encourage immediate action.

- **Why It Matters:** Time-limited offers can prompt clients to act quickly to avoid missing out.

- **Techniques:** Set a specific deadline for the offer and communicate the benefits of acting within the timeframe.

Example: I offered a discount that was only valid until the end of the week. By emphasizing the limited timeframe, I created urgency and encouraged the client to make a decision quickly, resulting in a successful close.

8.11 The Trial Close

The Trial Close involves testing the client's readiness to buy before attempting to close the sale.

- **What It Is:** A technique that gauges the client's interest and readiness to move forward.

- **Why It Matters:** It helps identify any remaining objections and ensures the client is ready to commit.

- **Techniques:** Ask questions like "How do you feel about this solution?" or "Is there anything else you need to know before we proceed?"

Example: I asked a client, "How do you feel about the proposal so far?" Their positive response indicated they were ready to move forward, and I proceeded with the direct close to finalize the sale.

8.12 The Incentive Close

The Incentive Close offers an additional benefit or incentive to encourage the client to commit.

- **What It Is:** A technique that sweetens the deal with extra value.

- **Why It Matters:** Incentives can tip the balance in your favor and motivate the client to act.

- **Techniques:** Offer discounts, free add-ons, or other bonuses as incentives.

Example: I offered a client a free month of service if they signed up by the end of the day. This incentive added extra value and encouraged the client to commit, leading to a successful close.

Chapter 9: Overcoming Objections

"Sales are contingent upon the attitude of the salesman, not the attitude of the prospect." - W. Clement Stone

9.1 Identifying Common Objections

Knowing the common objections helps you prepare and respond effectively.

- **What It Is:** Recognizing the typical concerns prospects have about your product or service.
- **Why It Matters:** Anticipating objections allows you to address them proactively.
- **Techniques:** Compile a list of common objections and develop responses for each.

Example: Price, implementation time, and return on investment are a few of the most common objections I hear. Knowing in advance which questions will surface, I prepared responses and case studies that covered each point. For example, when one prospect objected to the amount of time the implementation would take – citing the experience of a friend whose system took far too long – I provided a project timeline and the success stories of several other clients who'd implemented well within the stated timeframe.

9.2 Preparing Responses

Having prepared responses ensures you can address objections confidently and convincingly.

- **What It Is:** Developing well-thought-out responses to common objections.
- **Why It Matters:** Prepared responses help you stay composed and provide clear, confident answers.
- **Techniques:** Create a response guide and practice delivering them.

Example: I prepared detailed cost-benefit analyses to address price objections (showing that our solution would save money over the long term and have a big ROI) and I prepared a demo and simple user guide to address product complexity objections (to show that our solution was easy to use). As each objection came up, I could show potential clients my data and walk them through it.

9.3 Active Listening Techniques

Active listening helps you understand the underlying concerns behind objections.

- **What It Is:** Giving full attention to what the prospect is saying so that you can understand better what's on their mind.

- **Why It Matters:** Demonstrates empathy and ensures you address the real issue.

- **Techniques:** Listen without interrupting, repeat back what you heard, and ask clarifying questions.

Example: When the client raised concerns regarding implementation, I listened and relayed back their concerns to verify that I understood: "Our process for implementation is tried-and-tested, and our average downtime for our clients is considerably less than one percent." Their main concern was about downtime. After the client affirmed the downtime issue, I followed up: "We will complete the implementation in no more than one week." I was then able to alleviate their specific worries: "However, speak to your customers now and ask them if their companies had downtime the day they got our product. Ask them, was it more than one percent?"

9.4 Empathy in Objection Handling

Showing empathy helps build trust and rapport when handling objections.

- **What It Is:** Understanding and acknowledging the prospect's concerns and emotions.

- **Why It Matters:** Builds trust and shows that you genuinely care about their needs.

- **Techniques:** Use empathetic language and validate their concerns.

Example: "I totally understand why you're saying that. New software can be a bit intimidating. I know many of our clients have said the same thing before." I used the above empathy tool to ease a phone discussion with a client who was frustrated that we had to retrain his CEO since they were new to our software. After this conversation, he actually emailed to say how relieved he was to be working with me. Later, in a meeting, I told the client a story about a time when I was first learning to use software, how I struggled with it just like they were, and then went on to master it.

9.5 Providing Clear Solutions

Offering clear, actionable solutions helps resolve objections effectively.

- **What It Is:** Addressing objections with specific, practical solutions.

- **Why It Matters:** Demonstrates your problem-solving ability and reassures the prospect.

- **Techniques:** Provide detailed plans, examples, and next steps.

Example: For a client who was wary about integration with their existing systems – and used that concern as an argument against switching – I responded with documented integration roadmaps that detailed the integration timeframe and technical support available to facilitate the process. For a client who was fearful about data security, I described our data protection model and provided case studies of clients in the same industry who had successfully introduced our product with no issues.

9.6 Leveraging Testimonials

Using testimonials from satisfied clients can help overcome objections by providing social proof.

- **What It Is:** Sharing success stories and positive feedback from other clients.

- **Why It Matters:** Testimonials add credibility and show that others have had positive experiences.

- **Techniques:** Include relevant testimonials in your presentations and discussions.

Example: "I honestly thought this would not work." The prospect asked me if I had a testimonial from another client at their same size who was trying to do the same thing at a similar scale. "Sure, let me send that over to you now. It was a company similar in size to yours that did this thing at that scale, and they ended up increasing efficiency by 30 percent, and they have been using it for two years now."

9.7 Addressing Price Concerns

Handling price objections involves demonstrating value and ROI.

- **What It Is:** Answering the question of whether it's worth the investment by pointing to return and value.

- **Why It Matters:** Helps prospects see the long-term benefits and justify the expense.

- **Techniques:** Use cost-benefit analysis, ROI calculations, and flexible payment options.

Example: For a price-conscious prospect: I prepared an ROI breakdown illustrating the profit they'll make with my solution over the investment period, so that it was clear that my solution would positively impact their bottom line within the first year and continue to save money in the long term. Meanwhile, I offered a monthly payment plan to ease the investment for the organization. In another case, I broke down the price into monthly saved dollars per month, so that it was clear that they'll see a return on their investment within the year.

9.8 Building Confidence

Building confidence in your product and yourself helps alleviate objections.

- **What It Is:** Demonstrating your expertise and the reliability of your product.

- **Why It Matters:** Confidence reassures prospects and helps them feel secure in their decision.

- **Techniques:** Provide credentials, share success stories, and speak confidently.

Example: When a different client was questioning our ability to produce the desired outcome, I laid out my credentials and prior engagements with similar clients and their successful outcomes, which built confidence in us and allowed me to overcome his objections. I was also able to offer to introduce him to one of our happy clients that he could talk to directly, which helped to seal the deal.

9.9 Handling Last-Minute Objections

Addressing last-minute objections can be crucial to closing the deal.

- **What It Is:** Responding to objections that arise just before the final decision.

- **Why It Matters:** Last-minute objections can derail a sale if not handled properly.

- **Techniques:** Stay calm, listen carefully, and address the concerns directly.

Example: At the point of closing the deal with a client, he raised the expression of concern regarding the timeline. I remained calm to address their concern, realized the concern of the client, and provided him with a project plan to explain how I planned to deliver the project on time. This eased his concern and sealed the deal. Meanwhile, one of the clients was about to close the deal with us, but an urgent budget review led to hesitation from his side; to speed up the closure, I couched that it's possible to provide a temporary discount to fall within his immediate budget.

9.10 Using Data to Overcome Objections

Using data and evidence can help substantiate your claims and overcome objections.

- **What It Is:** Presenting factual information to support your responses to objections.

- **Why It Matters:** Data provides objective proof and can make your argument more convincing.

- **Techniques:** Use case studies, statistics, and performance metrics.

Example: If a prospect challenged the stability of our solution, I might pull out published performance metrics and case studies from clients who've used it over time and know to expect it to have 99.9 percent uptime. If a prospect questions your ability to support them as they scale up, you might present detailed usage data about how your solution has worked for existing clients that are already much larger.

97

9.11 Role-Playing Objections

Practicing objection handling through role-playing can improve your skills and confidence.

- **What It Is:** Simulating objection scenarios with a colleague or coach.

- **Why It Matters:** Helps you prepare for real-life objections and refine your responses.

- **Techniques:** Regularly practice with different scenarios and feedback sessions.

Example: I get my team to role-play scenarios in which they play each person's part – they get to be the client making an objection and I get to be the salesperson responding. Doing that has helped us all anticipate certain objections. We'd heard so many people push back on rising prices that when it happened with the next potential customer, we knew what to say. We'd practiced scenarios in which customers didn't know how to install devices and alarms they'd paid a lot of money for, as well as a whole host of more benign technical and service concerns. All of that prepared us for objections that might come up in real life.

9.12 Turning Objections into Opportunities

While objections are often seen as the enemy, these are actually the very things that will help you to develop your relationships with clients and enhance your offer.

- **What It Is:** Using objections as an opportunity to show value and address the need beneath the surface.

- **Why It Matters:** Addressing their concerns allows you to turn a reluctant prospect into a committed client.

- **Techniques:** Listen, get to the actual point at issue, and use an objection as a teaching moment.

Example: When a client complained about the complexity of our software, I answered with some suggested training sessions and a wealth of training resources ("Which one would you like as a starting point?") to not only solve the client's problem but to also stay true to our value proposition. Sometimes a worried client creates an objection ("I'm concerned about the ongoing support"). I would turn this into an opportunity with me answering definitively ("We have a world-class customer service, and my colleague X will be your dedicated account manager from now on if we work together – which one of those two answers do you like?"). And voilà! Sometimes a perceived objection can be turned into ruddy enthusiasm.

Conclusion

Becoming a master of advanced high-ticket remote closing techniques such as the assumptive close, urgency close, and the takeaway close are all crucial abilities to rely on as you move through your sales call, confidently taking your prospect right to that desired decision. The same can be said for the objection. Master techniques to prepare yourself for the most common objections and the techniques to deal with them in a positive and helpful way. The time-honored and most effective way to overcome buyers' objections is to show empathy, give a clear and positive solution or solution cycle, and provide them with the data to make the right decision. Not making a sale with empathy and data is not so much a failure on the part of the salesperson as the failure of the individual to trust themselves and rely purely on their subjective and emotional experience.

Secondly, we'll cover the topic of how to keep your clients for the long term and maximize the value they give throughout their relationship with your business. Let's get going.

Chapter 10: High-Ticket Case Studies

"Success is not just about making money. It's about making a difference." - Unknown

10.1 Success Story: John's Transformation

John is but one example. Here is his story. John had been a low-conversion-rate sales rep but, with his conversion rate skyrocketing because of his mastery of high-ticket closing concepts, he became one of the top sales reps in a Fortune-100 technology company. Because he was not closing many of the sales prospects that came along, John would have to work super-long hours to make quota. He approached our advanced training with trepidation, good for a dose of real-world pragmatism, not sure he would be able to make the conversion concepts 'fit'. John would complain regularly about 'the usual pedestrian nature of his average prospects' and find himself relating those complaints, with a mix of self-pity and frustration, into the abyss of the early morning sky. 'I came really close to quitting,' he told me a couple of months ago, before I had to leave for the airport, 'I was just over being one of the average sales guys, I was convinced those training courses were not right for me, but I am glad that I stuck with it because it sure beats having to schmooze with a bunch of dull prospects.' I can't speak for my siblings, but for my part I didn't stumble upon most of the concepts that are contained in the training courses – I persisted and learned. And I would do it all again.

10.2 Overcoming Challenges: Sarah's Journey

With a pack of objections and no precise place for destiny to excitedly land itself, Sarah found herself in a new role as a remote closer and facing a considerable amount of non-responsive inquiries, situations, and rejections. During our first coaching session, Sarah was glum due to rejections she faced on a daily basis as most of the high-end prospective clients she pitched to were either in the vacillation mode or were constantly sending rejections. Over a span of seven weeks, we worked in a more persistent way of targeting clients, using empathy emotions to physically sense their objections, deal with objections properly, expand the rapport method into objection handling, until she started practicing active listening, threw in some personalized follow-ups – this whole set of daily tasks bridged the gap, while building trust along the way and eventually scooping her first deal of $50,000 via the phone. The journey was truly endearing, seeing Sarah learn the ropes of persisting in rejections with the fundamental key to staying diligent in the marketplace, continuing to learn and eventually believing in herself.

10.3 Building a Client Base: Emma's Strategy

Emma was a remote closer in the financial services industry, and she picked up clients by reaching out to them personally and following up consistently. Emma and I drafted strengths-based, personalized proposals for her clients, addressing issues they felt were important, and scheduled bi-weekly follow-ups with them. In a year's time, Emma grew her client portfolio by 60 percent. As we built her follow-up routine together, each client felt connected, believed Emma heard their concerns, and felt understood. Personalized engagement and follow-up, I'm confident, led to a steady stream of incoming business.

10.4 Breaking Records: Mike's Achievements

Mike set the company's record for the most high-ticket deals he closed in a quarter. He told me his pitches began working even better once he got more comfortable with the power of the alternative close and urgency close. Mike made a record $500,000 in one quarter using those closing strategies. His ability to present options and create urgency was impeccable. Mike's story demonstrates the power of combining multiple closing strategies well, and the ability to adapt strategies, depending on the client.

10.5 From Struggle to Success: Karen's Path

Karen's confidence was shot, and she'd been rejected many times in the early days of her career. I recall the sessions were very much focused on working on her confidence through the power of preparation and positive affirmations, and also the usage of data through the clear presentation of ROI to combat any objections presented by her clients, and the adaptation of the approach being taken, with the clients having to 'earn' the discounts offered. Karen is now the top producer in the company, closing a deal of $100,000, transforming her career and way of life to boot. Karen's story highlights that to be top of your game in high-ticket sales, you have to develop a mastery in mindset and strategy.

10.6 Leveraging Technology: Tom's Approach

Leveraging CRM – customer relationship management – software and automation tools, Tom began using technology to filter, sort, and automate his workflow. I helped Tom develop a data-analytics strategy to track client behavior and refine his sales approach. Armed with the new efficiencies, Tom's average number of calls made before closing a deal dropped from 16 to six. He began closing more transactions, boosting his business by 30 percent. By the time he sold his company to a private-equity firm, he was generating nearly $1 million in revenue with a team of only six people, doing business in over 60 countries. Tom's success is so impressive, even Fortune has written about his team. And yet there are still plenty of salespeople in high-ticket industries who haven't caught up with the times. However, anyone who does start to incorporate tech into his sales structure can seize the lead for himself.

10.7 Client Retention: Lisa's Techniques

Lisa focused heavily on client retention, engaging in exceptional post-sale relationship management that included follow-up, support, and celebration of client successes. In one instance, I remember coaching Lisa on a client retention plan with customized touchpoints and added value.

We outlined various ways to engage meaningfully with her top clients. I'm proud to say that this approach worked beautifully, with a 90 percent client retention rate and a plethora of referrals. Lisa's approach to client retention is a classic example of the high-touch, high-ticket model of sales. She had developed a great rapport with her high-value, risk-taking clients, and did not want to lose them after selling them her solutions. My conclusion from this experience is that nurturing relationships with clients over a long period of time is an essential aspect of selling for the high-ticket/high-touch market, along with the fact that sales don't end after the point of transaction. It is imperative for the high-touch, high-ticket seller to engage with their clients post-sale, adding value to the relationship and keeping it alive and vibrant.

10.8 Expanding Reach: Paul's Growth

By utilizing social media marketing and content marketing, Paul began to exponentially expand his network, with new clients flocking to him. Together, we developed a strategy that saw Paul share his successes, give insight into his industry, and connect with potential clients directly on social media, which sheds a lot more personality on the great work that he does. The strategy showed Paul to be a human being, instead of just a brand, and this resulted in a rise in highly nurtured leads. Paul's story is important because it demonstrates how a business can utilize digital marketing in the high-ticket sales world, and just how important it is to build a presence on the internet.

10.9 Industry-Specific Success

Different industries call for different approaches. Two extremes: real estate talks about location, location, location, and how much the house is worth. Technology, on the other hand, addresses different needs, such as innovation and ROI. Each time, my clients and I would need to work through what the audience (ie, the industry) is most interested in. By addressing and even catering to the unique needs of one's audience, success was usually won. After working with a couple of tech firms on presentations for pitches to high-ticket clients, my client learned to speak to the innovative angle and ROI of the software, and he won these clients over.

10.10 Lessons from Failures

Failures teach you lessons. In this case, a client who originally struggled to make sales directly correlated his failure to convert clients to a lack of follow-up. Only when he decided to consistently follow up did he experience a 70 percent increase in his conversion rate. I always tell my clients to think of failure as a way through. So much of the lesson in sales comes from learning from your failures and adapting your strategy. This client's turnaround is a prime example.

10.11 Innovations in High-Ticket Sales

Innovation is an important enabler for being successful in the context of high-ticket sales. For example, my client decided to integrate AI-powered chatbots in the initial interactions with clients which seemed to be helpful as it allowed him to efficiently qualify his leads and thus save time throughout the sales process. Not only that – it also increased his conversion rates by 25 percent which was a great result. Being open for new technologies and finding a new innovative way to enhance the sales process and make it more efficient was clearly a smart move.

10.12 Scaling Success

If the original salesperson, say in your company's Atlanta office, has generated sales success through the close – a sense of urgency – and the use of personalized communications, train your entire sales team in these strategies. The chance is high they will work for them in your Los Angeles office. The chance is still higher that your company will derive benefit from scaling sales success – by experiencing increased sales of high-ticket items, your company's bottom line will grow. I helped my client develop a training programme translating these strategies into company policy.

Chapter 11: Personal Development and Mindset

"Your life does not get better by chance, it gets better by change." - Jim Rohn

11.1 Developing a Growth Mindset

A must-have component of a growth mindset is the drive to embrace challenges, to 'let your success be measured not by the size of the problem, but by the size of your solutions' (Robert Pagliarini, author). Once a client developed this mindset, where she saw each pushback or objection on a proposal as an opportunity to pivot to another angle that would work better for a client, then she improved her sales performance very quickly. I often say that rather than seeing challenges as problems, see them as opportunities to learn and grow.

11.2 Setting and Achieving Goals

A key to successfully attaining these goals, is to keep them affordable, so this client's goal was to sell $200,000 in the next six months. You might ask: how do you do that? Again, the question is big and easily distracting so we did it the proverbial one mouthful at a time. Divide the goal into steps that have an equivalent timeframe of a week or a month. Once we established a baseline of what could be done, the client developed an action plan that utilized weekly snapshots to drive progress. We went through this process week after week. The client initially set targets that seemed a little too easy to hit, but then we began to increase or up the game every couple of weeks. In short order, the client far exceeded the initial goal and ended up having a very successful six months. One of the most powerful forces in the universe is when something you are determined to achieve is attached to a specific measurable goal.

11.3 Overcoming Self-Doubt

Getting beyond self-doubt requires building confidence through formulating a preparatory process and mantras or positive self-talk. I worked with one client who suffered from crippling self-doubt. We created daily affirmations to increase confidence when making sales calls and formulated a thorough preparation for each call, leading to greater confidence and higher closing rates. I showed him techniques for calming his anxiety, retaining his sense of well-being, and ultimately his success.

11.4 Staying Motivated

Together, you need to find the internal motivation to stay on track and be proud of any small wins that might appear along the way, without all the fixating on a speedometer that might decrease your motivation. One client I worked with kept interest up by focusing on his why: "I enjoy helping a client be successful. It's like parenthood. It takes a lot but when you close a deal, no matter the value, I am proud and that soon becomes the engine that keeps me going." Keeps the motivation charged and deliberate. You need to bring a prize with you. A reward or an action that you enjoy doing and is yours to use as a trophy for when you achieve the five minutes. Keeping the fuel in the tank by accepting small rewards frequently allowed my college graduate client to keep cruising and soon driving like a pro. He was keeping the pedal to the metal.

11.5 Continuous Learning

Learning never stops. I had a client who attended all the industry seminars he could, and was constantly browsing the web for training sessions and classes on new sales techniques. He made a commitment to learning, and it showed in his results. Over the course of several months, his closing rate grew by 30 percent, and he outpaced his targets. I challenged him to set aside two hours a week to invest in his professional growth. Over time, he saw that small investment grow into a huge improvement in his ability to perform.

11.6 Work-Life Balance

A way one should have work-life balance, which is extremely important if one aspires successes in long term. The client with a burnout has worked 24/7, which resulted in an imbalance between work and personal life. By establishing boundaries between each task, the client was able to attain a better work-life harmony. He felt better, and his performance improved, as work-life balance is crucial to become successful in the long term. Thus, to help him, the schedule offered a possibility to relax and enjoy hobbies, which shifted his perspective on how to spend his day and enjoy his time better.

11.7 Building Resilience

One way to build resilience is to bounce back from test reversals. The client mentioned had experienced many rejections along the way. Nevertheless, he saw each rejection as a stepping stone and a learning opportunity. He used the process of confronting what went wrong and then making adjustments until he reached a 95 percent closing rate. I coached on a number of practical exercises to help build resilience, including documentation activities such as making a list of past successes and things that give them a sense of optimism. This helped the client make it through some dark periods.

11.8 Celebrating Success

Success needs to be celebrated to reinforce positive behavior and increase motivation. When we worked with a client who took the time to celebrate every accomplishment, big and small, from clearing a plate to clinching a multimillion-dollar contract, she was able to maintain a positive attitude and continued motivation. Celebrations of success also provide fuel to keep up momentum and striving for the next goal. Establish a routine to recognize successes, and see motivation and confidence go through the roof.

11.9 Developing Leadership Skills

Sometimes, leadership skills are needed, such as how to guide the team toward progress. One client of mine took a leadership position in the latest project. They asked me for my help with developing leadership skills that would enable them to become mentors to their team and create a collaborative environment. As a result of the coaching, the team became more cohesive and effective. A few examples of leadership development coaching are:

- Teaching effective active listening.

- Delegating tasks effectively and finding the right people to do the right job.

- Guiding their team towards success.

11.10 Cultivating Discipline

The cultivation of discipline requires regular efforts over time. A client who developed a daily prospecting and follow-up regimen translated into improved performance week after week as they managed their daily activities and kept track of their follow-up. The discipline required to stay on top of daily activities can help you achieve your long-term goals. We built an organized schedule to include time for the things that were critical to their success and their consistency in following through helped improve their results.

11.11 Building Confidence

You simply get confident through practice. For example, one client developed real confidence in his sales pitch. He learned to spend time preparing for each call by reviewing his material, rehearsing his pitch and visualizing it (mentally reviewing how the interaction would go, and how well he would do). He also took some time after a call to reflect on it, identifying what he did well and what he would do differently next time. As he got more comfortable with his pitch, and saw more and more success, his confidence grew.

11.12 The Importance of Self-Care

Self-care leads to higher performance and self-care helps improve productivity and provide greater results. Due to regular exercise and mindfulness practices and also vocal and reflexology self-care, my client is calmer and able to stay focused at work. Self-care helps them keep the energy up and provides sustained performance. I prescribed a lot of self-care activities (see appendix 6) for my tasks that ensured good long-term well-being and also enabled my clients to perform better at their jobs.

Chapter 12: High-Ticket Remote Closing in Different Industries

"In a world that is constantly changing, adaptability is the key to success." - Unknown

12.1 Real Estate

In real estate, high-ticket closing focuses on property appraisal value, hotspots, and investment opportunities. My client successfully closed multi-million-dollar property deals after we wrote pitches highlighting those points and preparing market analyses. We wrote about why each property has a unique selling point and comes with great investment opportunity. Our pitches helped sales pitch to high-net-worth end buyers.

12.2 Technology and Software

Products and services in technology and software focus on innovation, ROI, and scalability, and high-ticket sales pitches need to reflect that. One client won huge contracts for software by showcasing how it could save time and money for a company in the long-term. We produced presentations that emphasized the use of cutting-edge technology and a proven long-term ROI on expensive investment.

12.3 Health and Wellness

In health and wellness, focusing on its value for well-being and better quality of life is critical. An e-commerce client in this space closed high-ticket deals by focusing on helping their clients finally and notably improve their health and lifestyle through the products and services they offered. Marketing materials were peppered with testimonials and case studies of health outcome improvements, proof that formed the basis of clients' buying decisions.

12.4 Financial Services

Financial services demand proof of dependability, safety, and a path of likely financial growth. He closed deals for very high-ticket clients with rock-solid financial plans outlining the realization of their goals. He showed them detailed financial projections and case studies of his clients' growing wealth that came with using his services.

12.5 Coaching and Consulting

In high-ticket professional services sales, this focus on transformation is crucial. One client realized significant sales by relaying stories from former clients and demonstrating the measurable impacts of their coaching services. We worked on developing narrative hooks that communicated prospective clients' transformations using real-world measurables, like weight loss and positivity percentage.

12.6 Education and Training

In both education and training, it's the knowledge gained, the skills acquired, that are the '40-metre-pass' cases. During the development of one client's high-ticket training programmes, they had been struggling to close the deal due to concerns about the tangibility of the value they were offering. In their pitch, they would often focus on 'the science', which didn't resonate with their potential clients. So, one of our initiatives was to develop marketing collateral featuring real-life stories of past graduates of their programmes, and highlighting the tangible benefits they received from the programmes.

12.7 Luxury Goods

Marketing luxury goods revolves around the concept of aspirational imagery and exclusivity and quality. One of my clients in the luxury sector increased multiple-six-figure sales by focusing on the craftsmanship and features that made his product different from the rest. We crafted a narrative surrounding his brand that emphasized how exclusive and better quality his goods were.

12.8 Professional Services

Professional services companies need to prove that they can deliver results. A client sold hundreds of thousands of dollars of high-ticket consulting services by sending the prospect case studies and testimonials that proved they could generate results. We crafted detailed case studies that provided the context, described the problem, and showed the results.

12.9 E-commerce

High-ticket sales in any e-commerce follow protocol as generally the product quality, customer service and purchasing process play key roles. Once, my client focused on marketing a particular product without much information about the product which led to a drop in sales. We stepped into this situation and provided quality product information, personalized customer services and easy checkouts and super-efficient process to make possible high sales. We got involved by working on the website to provide more details about the product and sequence the content more as customers near to checkout and we also worked on customer service protocols to provide service just like these customers are in our personal shop! This was done considering the fact that a premium shopping experience inspires high-cost purchases.

12.10 Manufacturing

Efficiency, quality, and speed are important in manufacturing, and your client has options for customizing products that would work for the client. And large-scale buyers are invested in the way your client makes the products, as those features speak to the manufacturing of houses more broadly and their commitment to quality. You developed presentations for your client that focused on the manufacturing processes as being state of the art, and on the way their houses could be customized to fit the client's specific needs and space.

12.11 Hospitality and Travel

To sell high-end hospitality and travel, it is important to romanticize the experience and stress unique offerings. My client closed numerous six-figure luxury travel packages by emphasizing that his experience and service were unique and exclusive. We wrote marketing pieces emphasizing the unique, exclusive experiences available only to this client's buyers and guests. His selling point was the exclusivity of his tours and personal touches.

12.12 Non-Profit and Social Enterprises

In many non-profit or social enterprise contexts, what's critically important is the impact and sustainability of your programme – are you actually changing things, and will your work make a long-term difference? The client won big-ticket donors and partnerships by leading with concrete examples of positive impact and sustainable change. We wrote powerful impact reports and success stories that touched donors' and partners' hearts with meaningful difference they could make.

Conclusion

These chapters dive deep into high-ticket sales strategies, personal development, and industry-specific approaches to help you learn from success stories, develop a growth mindset, and understand different industries so you can fine-tune your skills and get extraordinary results with high-ticket remote closing. No matter what industry you're working in, if you have the right strategies, the right mindset, and tools as you try to master a new selling skill, you can take your sales game to the next level.

Chapter 13: Lead Generation Strategies

"The aim of marketing is to know and understand the customer so well the product or service fits him and sells itself." - Peter Drucker

13.1 Content Marketing

Content marketing involves creating valuable content to attract and engage potential clients.

- **What It Is:** Creating blogs, articles, videos, and more for readers and viewers that is useful or entertaining.

- **Quality is king.** Context-specific well-written content will position you as an expert in your field and draw organic traffic.

- **Techniques:** Create informative blog posts, engaging videos, and insightful infographics.

Example: A software client asked me to write a series of blog posts aimed at answering the most common issues in their target market. Once those pieces were live, they saw more website visitors and higher credibility, both of which led to an organic traffic increase of 30 percent within three months, and a significant jump in lead inquiries.

13.2 Social Media Marketing

I personally used marketing on social media as a means of reaching out to new clients on platforms such as LinkedIn, Facebook, or Instagram.

- **How It's Done:** The first and most obvious strategy is to use it as an avenue to re-post content and interact with interested followers. Social media platforms are great at promoting your services now, and they'll be excellent at it in the future.

- **Why It Matters:** Social media allows for direct access to potential customers as well as relationship-building.

- **Techniques:** Regular posting, engaging with comments, and using targeted ads.

Example: I helped a coaching industry client use LinkedIn to share testimonials and industry expertise. By posting organic content and engaging with their community regularly, their engagement grew by 25 percent, and because the content was so excellent, they earned high-quality leads – many of whom became clients.

13.3 Email Campaigns

Email campaigns are a powerful tool for nurturing leads and keeping your audience engaged.

- **What It Is:** A periodic email sent to a list of subscribers with tips, special offers, and news.

- **Benefit:** Keeps your brand on top of mind, paired with bottom-of-funnel messaging.

- **Why It Matters:** Keeps your brand on top of mind, paired with bottom-of-funnel messaging.

- **Techniques:** Create segmented email lists, personalize emails, and use compelling subject lines.

Example: Here's an example that also shows off how you can practice the principle of FOCUS: I was the client of a health and wellness brand that was looking for a creative way to advertise its upcoming webinars. One suggestion I made was to create multiple email campaigns, each designed for a specific segment on their email list. For instance, if I signed up for the list because I was interested in a certain type of cooking, I should receive personalized emails that reflect subtopics I had previously chosen. Two months after implementing this strategy, we observed an increase of 15 percent in the number of webinars sign-ups.

13.4 Paid Advertising

Paid advertising entails promoting products on Google Ads, social media ads, among others, for the aim of expanding the target audience.

- **What It Is:** Purchasing ads to send traffic to your site or landing pages.

- **Why It Matters:** Will get you instant visibility and can be narrowly targeted to your target audience.

- **Techniques:** Use targeted keywords, create compelling ad copy, and track ROI.

Example: I helped develop a Google ads campaign for an ecommerce client by targeting high-converting keywords and saw a 30 percent increase in website traffic which drove more sales. We constantly checked the performance of the ads and optimized keywords and ad copy for the best ROI.

13.5 Networking and Referrals

Networking and referrals leverage personal connections and word-of-mouth to generate leads.

- **What It Is:** Building relationships and encouraging satisfied clients to refer others.

- **Why It Matters:** Through referrals, you get pre-qualified prospects who are more likely to convert than prospects who hear about your business through other means.

- **Techniques:** Attend industry events, join professional groups, and create a referral program.

Example: A client in the financial services sector was guided to go to local business networking events; from this, she received many projected connections, and business referrals. Her consistent follow-up of those contacts has continuously grown her client base.

13.6 Webinars and Workshops

Hosting webinars and workshops positions you as an expert and attracts potential clients.

- **What It Is:** A free or paid online workshop that helps your audience solve a problem or master a skill.

- **Why It Matters:** Engages prospects and demonstrates your expertise.

- **Techniques:** Promote the event, send multichannel invitations, provide valuable content, and then reach out to attendees to follow up.

Example: A client in education held a monthly webinar with a discussion on trends related to her business. Hundreds of people attended each webinar, resulting in hundreds of leads (customers identified through their interest). We followed up with leads offering more information and incentives, and after becoming aware of her specialty topic, let's say we closed 10 people as customers.

13.7 SEO and Organic Traffic

SEO (Search Engine Optimization) helps improve your website's visibility on search engines.

- **What It Is:** Optimizing your site and content so it turns up earlier in search results.

- **Why It Matters:** Higher visibility leads to more organic traffic and potential leads.

- **Techniques:** Use relevant keywords, optimize meta tags, and create high-quality backlinks.

Example: I took on a real estate client to help their website perform better in local SEO keywords. We worked on local-themed keywords, made the website faster and more user-friendly so it could rank higher in search engines faster, and outreached to other sites with good domain authority to earn backlinks. This brought in more organic traffic (40 percent more!) of qualified leads looking for living space in that local area.

13.8 Lead Magnets

Lead magnets offer something valuable in exchange for contact information.

- **What It Is:** Free resources like eBooks, whitepapers, or templates that prospects can download.
- **Why It Matters:** Captures leads and allows you to nurture them through email marketing.
- **Techniques:** Create high-value resources and promote them through various channels.

Example: I helped a consulting industry client create a detailed resource in the form of an industry report. They promoted it on their website and socials, and saw a huge influx of leads on their email list as a consequence, with the leads of high quality. The leads who downloaded that report were interested in what they offered in their consulting service.

13.9 Cold Outreach Techniques

Cold outreach targets people who've never even heard of your brand.

- **What It Is:** Directly contacting prospects via email, phone, or social media.

- **Why It Matters:** Initiates conversations and generates leads from new sources.

- **Techniques:** Personalize messages, research prospects, and follow up consistently.

Example: We helped a B2B client by first prospecting the right target companies and then by designing and deploying a cold email campaign where the messaging was personalized to each prospect's pain points and then providing a clear value prop. We successfully booked some meetings and ultimately gained some new business contracts.

13.10 Partnerships and Alliances

Forming partnerships and alliances with other businesses can expand your reach and generate leads.

- **What It Is:** Collaborating with complementary businesses to offer joint solutions.

- **Why It Matters:** Gives you access to more users and more insight into what you offer.

- **Techniques:** Identify potential partners, create mutual value propositions, and formalize agreements.

Example: I helped a software client join forces with a hardware vendor so together they could be a complete solution, ultimately generating more business leads and closing more deals. We produced joint marketing materials and hosted webinars together where their outreach was doubled.

13.11 Leveraging Influencers

Influencer marketing uses individuals with a large following to promote your products or services.

- **What It Is:** Partnering with influencers to reach their audience and build credibility.

- **Why It Matters:** Influencers help to broaden your customer base and connect you with an engaged audience.

- **Techniques:** Identify relevant influencers, create authentic partnerships, and track engagement.

Example: A luxury goods client of mine worked with a lifestyle influencer: We found a suitable influencer with an audience that matched the target market of the client. His audience were doctoral students in the same country whose parents had the income needed to afford the products the client had to offer. After publishing the content, the client's brand awareness jumped, and its high-quality traffic value also doubled.

13.12 Tracking and Measuring Lead Generation

Using tracking and measuring to assess which of your lead-generated efforts are working and which aren't is key.

- **What It Does:** Tools and analytics to discover how your lead-gen tactics are performing.

- **Why It Matters:** Provides insights that help optimize your efforts and increase ROI.

- **Techniques:** Use CRM systems, track key metrics, and regularly review performance data.

Example: I developed a structured tracking system for a financial services client and learned which marketing lead generation channels were most effective. Through this analysis, we were able to improve conversion rates and more efficiently allocate marketing spend.

Chapter 14: Crafting the Perfect Pitch

"Make a customer, not a sale." -
Katherine Barchetti

14.1 Understanding Your Audience

Understanding your audience is the first step to crafting a compelling pitch.

- **What It Is:** Knowing who your audience is, their needs, and what motivates them.

- **Why It Matters:** A well-understood audience makes it easier to tailor your pitch effectively.

- **Techniques:** Conduct market research, create buyer personas, and gather feedback.

Example: I once took Tech Maven, an idea client who was trying to get her company's business software into a specific space, and developed a full profile of prospective buyers, how they used software like hers, what pain points they had, and what they needed to hear to buy. We then adjusted the way we crafted pitches to match what she would hear on the street. What this meant, I explained, was that she would get, on average, 35 percent of the engagement for each pitch. Because understanding her buyers as humans, not wallets on legs, had made the pitch more relevant and compelling.

14.2 Structuring Your Pitch

A well-structured pitch keeps your audience engaged and conveys your message clearly.

- **What It Is:** Grouping concepts and information into a logical flow that will attract, maintain, and compel your audience.

- **Why It Matters:** A good structure will make your pitch more persuasive, as well as easier to understand.

- **Techniques:** Hook, outline, call to action.

Example: I worked with a client in the financial industry to sculpt their pitch to ensure they began with a statistics-based hook about financial security, moved to a specific and thorough explanation of their unique solutions, and ended with a clear and actionable takeaway. That way, they could ensure their pitch made the most impact and closed the deal.

14.3 Highlighting Key Benefits

Highlighting key benefits shows your audience the value of your offering.

- **What It Is:** Besides pointing out the most important features and benefits and showcasing these items as solutions to the reader's problems.

- **Why It Matters:** Benefits resonate more with prospects than features.

- **Techniques:** Use benefit statements, customer testimonials, and case studies.

Example: One health client leveraged customer testimonials to illustrate the benefit of their wellness programmes to prospects. When she included before-and-after photos and examples of actual results, it proved that other customers benefited, which made the benefit more real and was a key factor in getting more interest and sales.

14.4 Using Visual Aids

Visual aids can make your pitch more engaging and easier to understand.

- **What It Is:** Incorporating visuals like slides, charts, and videos to complement your message.

- **Why It Matters:** Visuals help break down complex information and keep the audience engaged.

- **Techniques:** Use clear, high-quality visuals that support your key points.

Example: We created a presentation deck with charts and videos for a client in the education industry. That made their pitch more lively and easy to grasp. Later, the presenters reported their presentation was better received and attended, with better recall and retention from the audience.

14.5 Practicing Delivery

Practicing your delivery ensures you present your pitch confidently and smoothly.

- **What It Is:** Rehearsing your pitch multiple times to refine your delivery.

- **Why It Matters:** Confidence and a steady delivery can make a big difference to your pitch.

- **Techniques:** Practice in front of a mirror, record yourself, and seek feedback.

Example: Advance preparation helped me get my pitch to that level – tone, pace, body language – and then, when I actually was delivering it live, I felt more confident and that confidence in turn led to greater conversion of that pitch.

14.6 Personalizing Your Pitch

Personalizing your pitch makes it more relevant and impactful to your audience.

- **What It Is:** Crafting a message that you tailor to specific needs and interests of your audience.

- **Why It Matters:** What's more persuasive than a pitch that sounds like it was made just for you? The fact it obviously was.

- **Techniques:** Research your audience, reference specific needs, and use personalized examples.

Example: I successfully supported one contract negotiator who worked for a software client company, by researching the issues each prospect client faced, and personalizing the pitches accordingly. This increased personalization resulted in substantially improved engagement and conversion rates.

14.7 Handling Questions

Handling questions effectively during your pitch shows your expertise and builds trust.

- **What It Is:** Being prepared to answer questions confidently and accurately.

- **Why It Matters:** Addressing questions effectively can alleviate concerns and reinforce your message.

- **Techniques:** Anticipate common questions, prepare clear responses, and remain calm.

Example: Before pitching a client in the financial services industry, we had a plan for answering questions about regulatory compliance beforehand. When these questions were raised, we were ready, answered the questions completely, and looked good doing it.

14.8 Closing with Confidence

Closing your pitch with confidence leaves a lasting impression and encourages action.

- **What It Is:** A powerful end to an argument that reasserts your message in an actionable way.

- **Why It Matters:** A confident close can influence the audience's decision-making process.

- **Techniques:** Summarize key points, restate the benefits, and include a clear call to action.

Example: I often coach a luxury goods client on closing his pitch by articulating the unique benefits that make his products worthwhile, and then ending with "and I'm asking you because I can see that you and I can make this happen together." This principle helps him get more positive responses, and more deals close.

14.9 Storytelling in Your Pitch

Incorporating storytelling into your pitch makes it more engaging and relatable.

- **What It Is:** Using stories to illustrate points and connect emotionally with your audience.

- **Why It Matters:** Stories are memorable and can make complex information easier to understand.

- **Techniques:** Share success stories, use relatable examples, and create a narrative arc.

Example: One coaching client I've worked with creates "case stories", sharing the positive impact their services have produced for clients. They list several clients, along with how the coach helped them create new jobs or international trade opportunities. Clients create emotions, and interested people will want to replicate the experience.

14.10 Addressing Objections Early

Addressing potential objections early in your pitch can preemptively alleviate concerns.

- **What It Is:** Premeditating objections from the audience and countering them.
- **Why It Matters:** Anticipating objections shows that you have thought about the issue and are ready to dispel them.
- **Techniques:** Highlight potential concerns and provide solutions or reassurances.

Example: For an enterprise software client, we had anticipated objections that our solution was too difficult to implement, so we presented early in the pitch our rapid onboarding and rock-solid support system as a way to cement these implementation concerns quickly, before they could become a larger concern.

14.11 Using Data to Support Your Pitch

Using data to support your pitch adds credibility and substantiates your claims.

- **What It Is:** Incorporating relevant data and statistics to back up your points.
- **Why It Matters:** Data-driven pitches are more persuasive and credible.
- **Techniques:** Use case studies, industry reports, and performance metrics.

Example: I've seen one pitch involving a client in the e-commerce space backed up by evidence of increased conversion rates and customer satisfaction, which seemed to really justify the goal. Those actual results helped make the pitch much more credible and trustworthy.

14.12 Adapting Pitches for Different Audiences

Adapting your pitch for different audiences ensures it resonates with everyone you're addressing.

- **What It Is:** Tailoring your pitch to the precise interests or needs of your different audience segments.

- **Why It Matters:** For the same energy expended, a custom pitch is more likely to entice and persuade a range of audiences.

- **Techniques:** Adjust your language, focus on relevant benefits, and customize examples.

Example: For one client in the education sector, we constructed three variations of a pitch, tailored to the needs of 'parents', 'teachers', and 'investors'; something that showcased distinct benefits for each group. And as a result, engagement surged, while effectiveness rose across all segments.

Chapter 15: Scaling Your Business

"Growth is never by mere chance; it is the result of forces working together." - James Cash Penney

15.1 Building a Sales Team

Building a competent sales team is essential for scaling your business.

- **What It Is:** Recruiting, training, and managing a team of sales professionals.

- **Why It Matters:** A strong sales team can significantly increase your reach and revenue.

- **Techniques:** Hire skilled salespeople, provide comprehensive training, and foster a collaborative culture.

Example: I worked with a client in the tech sector who was building a sales team from the ground up. Early on, we worked to hire candidates who possessed top-notch social skills, and then trained them extensively on our products and sales models. Initially, we saw a 50 percent increase in sales year over year. However, it was the collaborative nature of the team, driven by frequent team-building activities, often involving multiple teams in a collaborative setting, and open communication that really bolstered performance.

15.2 Automating Processes

Automating processes improves efficiency and frees up time for strategic activities.

- **What It Is:** Using technology to streamline repetitive tasks and workflows.

- **Why It Matters:** Automation ensures accuracy and frees your team up to concentrate on high-stakes work.

- **Techniques:** Implement CRM systems, automate email campaigns, and use project management tools.

Example: A company in the e-commerce industry developed a system to send automated emails to their customers, and based on their behavior, adjusted their follow-ups. They did this to save time and were able to achieve a 20 percent increase in conversions. In addition, we implemented a CRM for them which helped streamline their sales funnel on the go. Now, their sales team spends more time on closing deals and less on administrative tasks.

15.3 Expanding Your Reach

Expanding your reach involves entering new markets and reaching a broader audience.

- **What It Is:** Developing strategies to attract new customer segments and geographic markets.

- **Why It Matters:** Growth often requires tapping into new opportunities beyond your current market.

- **Techniques:** Conduct market research, adapt your offerings, and use targeted marketing.

Example: I worked with a client in the financial service industry who wanted to expand their reach, so I helped them penetrate the international market. Depending on the cultural sensitivities and legislations of the markets they wanted to access, their marketing strategies were customized accordingly, leading to a good market share penetration and a boosted revenue. Also, they introduced digital campaigns targeted at those regions. As a result, their brand awareness internationally has increased by 200 percent compared to what it was before.

15.4 Increasing Your Offerings

Increasing your offerings involves diversifying your products or services to attract more clients.

- **What It Is:** Expanding your product or service line to meet additional customer needs.

- **Why It Matters:** Diversification can reduce risk and open up new revenue streams.

- **Techniques:** Identify market gaps, develop complementary products, and test new offerings.

Example: A coaching-business client broadened their offerings to include online courses and workshops and thus attracted more clients and four more income streams, creating much greater stability than in the past. We conducted market research to determine where gaps existed and to then test the new offerings with pilot programs before going full scale.

15.5 Partnerships and Alliances

Forming strategic partnerships and alliances can accelerate your business growth.

- **What It Is:** Collaborating with other businesses to leverage each other's strengths.

- **Why It Matters:** Partnerships can provide access to new markets, resources, and expertise.

- **Techniques:** Identify potential partners, create win-win propositions, and formalize agreements.

Example: One of my clients in the healthcare sector started a strategic partnership with a supplier of wellness products in order to offer a complete health package. They doubled their outreach and increased their chances to win clients, thanks to a joint marketing activity involving articles and webinars we created together.

15.6 Leveraging Technology

Leveraging technology helps scale operations and improve efficiency.

- **What It Is:** Using advanced tools and systems to streamline processes and enhance performance.

- **Why It Matters:** Technology can automate tasks, provide insights, and facilitate growth.

- **Techniques:** Implement cloud solutions, use data analytics, and adopt cutting-edge tools.

Example: I helped a manufacturing client establish and implement an ERP system. This system helped reduce and improve the overall operations management, sector-related compliance, etc. It improved the current stock and future inventory management, increased productivity, and helped organizational growth. Also, we integrated a data-analytics tool to help the company analyze current real-time data and those from previous periods. This analytic software helped them understand the operations and make informed decisions.

15.7 Monitoring Performance

Monitoring performance ensures that your scaling efforts are effective and on track.

- **What It Is:** Regularly tracking key metrics to assess business performance.

- **Why It Matters:** Continuous monitoring helps identify areas for improvement and measure success.

- **Techniques:** Use performance dashboards, set KPIs, and conduct regular reviews.

Example: A tech client used performance dashboards to track sales units, customer satisfaction, market share, operational efficiency, and staff utilization in real time. With this information, key decisions could be made and strategies adjusted as required, ensuring continued growth. Every quarter, we would review performance with this client to determine if targets were on track or needed to be altered.

15.8 Continuous Improvement

Continuous improvement involves regularly refining processes and strategies to enhance performance.

- **What It Is:** Adopting a mindset of ongoing enhancement and adaptation.

- **Why It Matters:** Incremental improvements can lead to significant gains over time.

- **Techniques:** Conduct regular audits, gather feedback, and implement changes.

Example: Currently, I am coaching a hospitality client through a step-by-step process of improvement. Through a process of collecting guest feedback and conducting operational audits, they were able to make small but consistent changes to the quality of their experience for guests. This increased repeat business and allowed them to continue to grow their business. In addition, we set up a feedback loop for employees to record how they would improve things, so everyone in the organization felt confident that their ideas were valued and important.

15.9 Training and Development

Invest in training and development so that your team is ready for the challenges of scaling up.

- **What It Is:** Providing ongoing education and skill development for your employees.

- **Why It Matters:** A well-trained team can better execute a strategy, is more motivated and effective, and is more likely to foster growth.

- **Techniques:** Offer regular training sessions, encourage professional development, and provide resources.

Example: A professional services client rolled out an expansive program that covered workshops, online courses, boardroom leadership, and line-manager mentorship. This training has led to significant improvements in team performance and employee retention and helped us to scale. We actively encouraged attendance at industry conferences and seminars in order to boost the team's knowledge of trends.

15.10 Financial Planning

Financial planning is crucial for managing the costs associated with scaling your business.

- **What It Is:** Developing a detailed financial plan to support growth initiatives.

- **Why It Matters:** Ensures you have the necessary resources and can manage risks effectively.

- **Techniques:** Create budgets, forecast financial needs, and monitor cash flow.

Example: For one retail client, I helped her develop a financial plan to expand her presence with new stores. I generated forecasting scenarios for the costs involved to open stores, and then estimated the likely revenue potential in these new markets, which she used to acquire capital and manage the expansion effectively. We also created a financial dashboard to track all of this in real time, monitoring whether she was staying on track versus driving additional expenses so that we could correct course if needed.

15.11 Risk Management

Risk management involves identifying and mitigating potential risks that could impact your growth.

- **What It Is:** Proactively managing risks to minimize their impact on your business.

- **Why It Matters:** Reduces the likelihood of setbacks and ensures sustained growth.

- **Techniques:** Conduct risk assessments, develop contingency plans, and monitor risks.

Example: She formed a risk management plan for a client in the construction sector, consisting of regular safety audits and contingency planning for delayed projects, all tailored to reduce obstacles to growth. We also keep a lookout for potential new threats and work proactively to limit their damage on an ongoing basis with regular risk assessments.

15.12 Sustainable Growth Strategies

Sustainable growth strategies ensure your business can grow without compromising quality or resources.

- **What It Is:** Implementing practices that support long-term, sustainable growth.

- **Why It Matters:** Ensures your business can scale effectively and responsibly.

- **Techniques:** Focus on quality, manage resources efficiently, and plan for the long term.

Example: In work with another client in the environmental services sector, we discussed strategy for sustaining growth. Instead of focusing on an unsustainable pathway of heavy price cuts to drive business, we supported them in promoting quality and resource efficiency to maintain steady growth while staying true to their environmental ideals. Not only was this good for the environment, but it also allowed them to build a reputation for environmental sustainability that attracted more environmentally conscious clients.

Conclusion

These chapters walk you through time-tested lead gen strategies, the art of the perfect pitch, and scaling your business. More than just theory, implementing these tips can strengthen your sales efforts, better communicate with your team, and grow your business in the world of remote high-ticket closing. With the right approach and ongoing improvement, you can see mass success and amplify your business in any sphere.

Chapter 16: Metrics and Analytics

"Without data, you're just another person with an opinion." - W. Edwards Deming

16.1 Key Sales Metrics

You can't make good decisions without looking closely at your key sales metrics.

- **What It Is:** The vital statistics, such as revenue, average deal size and length of the sales cycle, that track aspects of your sales process.

- **Why It Matters:** Identifies strengths and weaknesses, guiding strategic decisions and improvements.

- **Techniques:** Regularly track and analyze metrics using CRM systems and performance dashboards.

Example: I worked with a client who was in the SaaS business. In their business, average deal size and length of sales cycle are important performance drivers. We found large deals took significantly more time to close. In response, we implemented a more structured follow-up process and provided potential clients with additional resources. We were able to reduce the sales cycle for our larger deals and, in turn, increase high-value revenue every quarter by 20 percent.

16.2 Tracking Lead Generation

Tracking lead generation metrics provides insights into which marketing efforts are most effective.

- **What It Is:** Measuring how many leads are created by such sources as a social media blast, an email campaign, or a webinar.

- **Why It Matters:** Figuring out the best way to reach leads so that there is a powerful yet cost-effective expenditure of resources.

- **Techniques:** Gather leads and figure out where they come from using Google Analytics; use your CRM to track conversions.

Example: Our client in the healthcare industry was tracking leads from channelled marketing sources. We learned that webinars were particularly effective – 40 percent of high-quality leads came from webinars. We then started to produce more webinars, or improved promotion efforts around webinars, and we saw a 30 percent increase in leads.

16.3 Conversion Rates

Conversion rates measure the percentage of leads that turn into paying customers.

- **What It Is:** The number of converted leads at a given point divided by that number of leads at the first step in the funnel.

- **Why It Matters:** Indicates the efficiency of your sales process and areas needing improvement.

- **Techniques:** Calculate conversion rates for different stages of the sales funnel to identify bottlenecks.

Example: A client wanted to improve their bottom line, so we went back to the acquisition stage and analysed their click-through and conversion rates at different stages of the sales process. Their proposal stage had a clearly identifiable drop-off, which was addressed by updating their proposal templates and training the sales team to be more responsive to client objections. We ended up boosting their conversion rate from 10 percent to 15 percent (about 50 percent increase).

16.4 Customer Acquisition Cost

Customer acquisition cost (CAC) measures the cost of acquiring a new customer.

- **What It Is:** Divide the total sales and marketing expenditure by the number of new customers you acquire.

- **Why It Matters:** Measuring your marketing activity against your business goals will help you assess if your customer acquisition efforts working or not, allowing you to refine your budget spend.

- **Techniques:** Keep track of marketing expenses, sales salaries and other costs to figure out your CAC properly.

Example: When a tech startup I worked with realised their CAC was much higher than they'd projected, I looked at their spending to see what could be streamlined. We reduced their digital ad spend and refined their email lead nurturing cycle, ultimately saving costs and reducing their CAC by 20 percent while maintaining lead quality.

16.5 Lifetime Value of a Customer

LTV is a prediction of how much revenue a customer will bring to your company during their lifetime as a customer.

- **What It Is:** The average revenue per customer multiplied by the customer lifespan.

- **Why It Matters:** Determines how much you can afford to pay to gain new customers, and guides marketing budgets.

- **Techniques:** Use historical data to estimate customer retention rates and average purchase values.

Example: We estimated the LTV for one of my clients, and it turned out that loyal customers were many times more valuable than just one-time customers. We implemented a customer loyalty programme with dedicated offers and communications that could be personalised, and our customer retention rose by 25 percent and their LTV exponentially.

16.6 Performance Dashboards

Performance dashboards provide a visual representation of your key metrics and analytics.

- **What It Is:** Tools that display important sales data in an easily digestible format.

- **Why It Matters:** Enables quick assessment of performance and informed decision-making.

- **Techniques:** Use software like Tableau, Power BI, or CRM systems to create interactive dashboards.

Example: I built a performance dashboard for a client to track some of the most important metrics for their business, for example, sales pipeline, conversion rates of leads, and quarterly revenue forecasts, which they could monitor in real time. This enabled them to make more data-focused decisions much more quickly than before, and as a result, we were able to improve overall performance by 15 percent.

16.7 Analyzing Sales Data

Analyzing sales data involves examining metrics to gain insights and improve strategies.

- **What It Is:** Reviewing sales figures, trends, and patterns to understand performance.

- **Why It Matters:** Identifies areas for improvement and opportunities for growth.

- **Techniques:** Use data analytics tools to perform in-depth analysis and generate actionable insights.

Example: The analysis of sales data showed a decline in conversions during the holiday season. Using seasonal promotions and individual outreach, we increased holiday sales by 25 percent the next year.

16.8 Using Analytics to Improve

Using analytics to improve means leveraging data insights to enhance your sales process.

- **What It Is:** Applying findings from data analysis to optimize strategies and operations.

- **Why It Matters:** Helps refine processes and increase efficiency, leading to better results.

- **Techniques:** Implement changes based on data-driven insights and continuously monitor the impact.

Example: One of my clients asked me to analyse their sales calls with prospect customers using software that analysed the audio for their use of language. By looking at objections that came up and weaker segments of the pitch, we developed better scripts and training for the team that have increased the close rate by 15 percent.

16.9 Forecasting Sales

Forecasting sales involves predicting future sales based on historical data and trends.

- **What It Is:** Forecast of future sales revenues and performance to guide planning and resource allocation.

- **Why It Matters:** Helps with budgeting, inventory management, and setting realistic targets.

- **Techniques:** Use historical sales data, market analysis, and predictive modeling to create accurate forecasts.

Example: One retail client that used sales forecasting before the holiday season reduced stockouts and overstaffing, subsequently lowering costs and maximising profitability.

16.10 ROI Calculation

ROI (Return on Investment) measures the profitability of your sales and marketing efforts.

- **What It Is:** The percentage return on investment in net profits.

- **Why It Matters:** Determines the effectiveness of your investments and guides future spending.

- **Techniques:** Calculate ROI for each campaign; compare results to find the most lucrative strategies.

Example: An email marketing client needed to prove the ROI of their email marketing program, but felt they were being spread too thinly. We examined the results to see what was working and concentrated on continuing those tactics, thereby driving up the efficiency of their marketing efforts for increased ROI of exactly 20 percent.

16.11 Benchmarking Against Industry Standards

Benchmarking involves comparing your performance metrics to industry standards.

- **What It Is:** Evaluating how your business measures up to competitors and industry norms.

- **Why It Matters:** Provides insights into areas for improvement and helps identify growth opportunities.

- **Techniques:** Use industry reports and data to benchmark your metrics against peers.

Example: A client in the SaaS industry used benchmarking to compare their customer satisfaction scores to industry standards. By identifying areas where they were underperforming, we implemented targeted improvements that resulted in a 10-point increase in customer satisfaction and a 20-point increase in customer loyalty over a four-year period.

16.12 Data-Driven Decision Making

Data-driven decision-making involves using data insights to guide business decisions.

- **What It Is:** Making strategic choices based on data analysis and evidence.

- **Why It Matters:** Enhances rationality, improves decision soundness, and lowers risk levels.

- **Techniques:** Incorporate data analysis into your decision-making process and regularly review performance data.

Example: I assured one customer that data-based decision making could facilitate their product launch – by conducting a trend analysis of market development and prospects of the product, and sharing customer-reported feedback, we helped them launch new products that fulfilled market demand, and sales also grew rapidly since then, improving their market position.

153

Chapter 17: Overcoming Sales Slumps

"Every strike brings me closer to the next home run." - Babe Ruth

17.1 Identifying the Cause

Identifying the cause of a sales slump is the first step to overcoming it.

- **What It Is:** Analyzing factors that contribute to a decline in sales performance.

- **Why It Matters:** Understanding the root cause helps develop effective solutions and strategies.

- **Techniques:** Review sales data, gather feedback, and identify patterns that indicate the underlying issues.

Example: A client who experienced a drop in sales reviewed his data and realized that a modification to his pricing policy was the culprit. We made changes to the pricing model to better align with the market expectations and sales rebounded, as did customer satisfaction.

17.2 Adjusting Strategies

Adjusting strategies involves tweaking your approach based on identified issues and market conditions.

- **What It Is:** Adapting tactics to fit current market conditions and customer needs.

- **Why It Matters:** Flexibility in strategy can help overcome obstacles and improve performance.

- **Techniques:** Implement new sales techniques, revise marketing plans, and optimize operational processes.

Example: An IT client began to lose market share to cheaper competitors. Following his Unlocking Success Session, he innovated a new sales strategy that shifted his focus to a different (and more profitable) market, turning around the slump to increase sales 20 percent for his company within six months.

17.3 Staying Positive

Staying positive during a sales slump is crucial for maintaining motivation and morale.

- **What It Is:** Maintaining a positive mindset despite challenges and setbacks.

- **Why It Matters:** Positivity helps you stay focused, resilient, and motivated to find solutions.

- **Techniques:** Recite positive affirmations, celebrate small victories, and maintain team morale.

Example: Responding to a client with a sales slump that had gone on for some time, I told him: keep positive, ensure you celebrate the small successes, and create a culture within your team of supporting each other as best you can. Morale will improve and the longer-term team resilience will result in a gradual improvement in performance.

17.4 Seeking Feedback

Feedback from customers and colleagues can provide valuable insights into your reasons for experiencing sales slumps.

- **What It Is:** Gathering input from various sources to understand issues and identify solutions.

- **Why It Matters:** Feedback offers a different perspective and helps improve strategies and processes.

- **Techniques:** Conduct surveys, hold feedback sessions, and encourage open communication.

Example: One retail client asked team members and customers for feedback about their product presentation and customer service. Feedback about package presentations and personalised customer service indicated training and display technique improvements were needed. After the improvements were made, sales increased and customer satisfaction also increased.

17.5 Training and Development

Investing in training and development can help improve skills and overcome sales slumps.

- **What It Is:** Keeping your sales team's skills and knowledge up to date through ongoing learning.
- **Why It Matters:** Well-trained salespeople are more effective, confident, and motivated.
- **Techniques:** Offer workshops, online courses, and mentorship programs tailored to specific needs.

Example: With this client I developed a comprehensive sales training program for their sales team that included a focus on advanced closing techniques and customer relationship management. As a result of this investment, not only did the team improve performance levels, but the organisation was able to break a sales slump and increase their close rate by 15 percent.

17.6 Re-engaging Leads

Re-engaging leads involves reconnecting with potential clients who previously showed interest but didn't convert.

- **What It Is:** Calling leads who'd gone cold to try to get them back on track.

- **Why It Matters:** Revives interest and can lead to conversions that were previously lost.

- **Techniques:** Use personalized emails, offer new incentives, and follow up consistently with relevant content.

Example: This client reappeared on the scene with the help of a targeted email campaign – offering some customers a time-limited discount, and another group personally-addressed follow-up messages. This kept old leads interested and ultimately generated several new sales: perhaps enough to get them out of the slump.

17.7 Setting New Goals

Setting new goals can provide direction and motivation during a sales slump.

- **What It Is:** Establishing fresh objectives to refocus efforts and measure progress.

- **Why It Matters:** New objectives can give new energy to an organisation, and can establish a course to a desired future.

- **Techniques:** Set SMART goals (Specific, Measurable, Achievable, Relevant, Time-bound) so they are realistic and motivating.

Example: With a client who was going through a sales drought, I set new targets and then segmented them into more achievable milestones, sparking increased effort among the team and leading to a dramatic rise in sales and a more energised workforce.

17.8 Celebrating Small Wins

Celebrating small wins can boost morale and motivation during tough times.

- **What It Is:** Recognizing and rewarding minor achievements and progress.

- **Why It Matters:** Positive reinforcement encourages continued effort and perseverance.

- **Techniques:** Celebrate achievements publicly, provide rewards, and acknowledge contributions regularly.

Example: With a client, we started tracking and celebrating small sales team milestones -– getting towards weekly targets, or new meetings set up – all of which increased morale and motivation as they came out of a sales slump and improved performance over time.

17.9 Analyzing Competitor Strategies

Analyzing competitor strategies can provide insights and inspiration to overcome sales slumps.

- **What It Is:** Looking at your competition to see what they're doing and learning from their techniques.

- **Why It Matters:** Insight that can identify new market opportunities and potential gaps in your own strategy.

- **Techniques:** Conduct competitive analysis, study market trends, and benchmark against competitors.

Example: A client in the tech industry analysed a competitor that was kicking their butt and reversed a sales slump by determining the key elements of its approach to product launches and marketing, and then adding a twist to resurrect their flagging sales with a 25 percent gain in market share.

17.10 Innovation and Creativity

Innovation and creativity can lead to new approaches and solutions during a sales slump.

- **What It Is:** Thinking outside the box to develop unique strategies and solutions.

- **Why It Matters:** Innovative ideas can differentiate your business and attract new customers.

- **Techniques:** Encourage brainstorming sessions, explore new technologies, and experiment with creative marketing.

Example: Thanks to my recommendations regarding feedback from customers and insights from the market, I supported a client in launching a new product feature. The update ignited a new life in the product portfolio of their company, and in the following quarter sales bounced back with a whopping 30 percent. A struggling client in such a case is suddenly calibrated and moving toward stability.

17.11 Collaborating with Your Team

Collaborating with your team can provide new perspectives and collective problem-solving.

- **What It Is:** Working together to address challenges and develop solutions collaboratively.

- **Why It Matters:** Collaboration sparks creativity, ensures that all the stakeholders are bought in, and allows the team to take advantage of multiple skills.

- **Techniques:** Hold regular team meetings, encourage idea sharing, and foster a collaborative culture.

Example: We had one client who encouraged his team of salespeople to conduct brainstorming sessions on a regular basis. These brainstorming sessions led the team to new ideas and strategies – something they hadn't tried before – which ultimately helped them get out of their sales rut and become more enthusiastic and productive.

17.12 Maintaining Consistency

Maintaining consistency in your efforts is crucial for long-term success, even during slumps.

- **What It Is:** Staying committed to your strategies and continuously putting in consistent effort.

- **Why It Matters:** Consistency builds momentum and leads to sustainable improvements over time.

- **Techniques:** Develop a routine, set regular check-ins, and track progress consistently.

Example: With one client, I offered the following advice. 'Try to keep to the same schedule for following up with leads,' I said. 'Even when things are slow, keep at it. Over time, you will see a steady increase in conversions, and you'll pull out of the sales slump.'

Chapter 18: Ethical Selling Practices

"Ethics is knowing the difference between what you have a right to do and what is right to do." - Potter Stewart

18.1 Importance of Ethics in Sales

Ethics in sales is critical for building long-term trust and maintaining a positive reputation.

- **What It Is:** Adhering to moral principles and professional standards in all sales activities.

- **Why It Matters:** 'Good men follow good men.' Ethical conduct increases trust, loyalty and repeat business. A brand that builds a reputation for ethical conduct builds reputation – and repeat business.

- **Techniques:** Commit to honesty, transparency, and fairness in all sales interactions.

Example: We had a client in the financial services sector who talked about 'sales with integrity', with some training courses focused on this idea. They increasingly focused on salespeople succeeding by being honest and open, creating relationships based on trust, in turn resulting in higher levels of client retention and referrals.

18.2 Building Trust with Integrity

Building trust through integrity means being honest and reliable in all your dealings.

- **What It Is:** Consistently demonstrating honesty, reliability, and accountability.

- **Why It Matters:** Trust is the foundation of long-lasting customer relationships and business success.

- **Techniques:** Always deliver on promises, admit mistakes, and provide accurate information.

Example: A client of mine placed a high importance on staying truthful and being open about the things their product did and did not do. This imparted trust within their clients, who appreciated the frankness in conveying the product's capabilities and were more likely to recommend the company.

18.3 Transparency in Communication

Transparency in communication involves being open and clear about all aspects of your offerings.

- **What It Is:** Providing all necessary information without hiding details or misleading clients.

- **Why It Matters:** Transparent communication prevents misunderstandings, builds credibility, and fosters trust.

- **Techniques:** Clearly outline pricing, terms, and conditions, and be upfront about potential drawbacks.

Example: In the context of internal control, a software client explained transparency in decision-making: 'We openly disclosed an itemised price-list for our product with all costs (taxes, transport, etc) quoted separately. During a sales pitch, we disclosed all features and the limitations associated with each, reducing post-sale wrangling.' In the long run, this approach contributed to increased referrals, greater customer satisfaction, and improved brand value.

18.4 Avoiding Misleading Tactics

Avoiding misleading tactics ensures that you provide accurate and truthful information to clients.

- **What It Is:** Refraining from exaggeration, false claims, or deceptive practices in sales.

- **Why It Matters:** Pulling one over on your clients can land you with dissatisfied customers, a damaged reputation, and a strong sense of karma.

- **Techniques:** Use factual information, avoid overpromising, and ensure all claims are verifiable.

Example: I helped a client steer away from making wild claims about what their product could do – such as 'Cure whatever ails you!' – and instead focused on proven benefits and real testimonials from customers. The experience of discovering truth created a more honest and credible brand image that the audience could trust.

18.5 Respecting Client Privacy

Respecting client privacy involves protecting their personal and business information from misuse.

- **What It Is:** Ensuring that client information is kept confidential and used appropriately.

- **Why It Matters:** Safeguarding privacy, your customers' information and your company from lawsuits, and embarrassing data breaches.

- **Techniques:** Implement data protection measures, secure consent for data usage, and follow privacy laws.

Example: Our client in the medical industry created strict data-protection rules that safeguarded patient information. This respect of privacy reflected in the trust of clients, growing their reputation as a trustworthy company, which resulted in increased retention and referrals.

18.6 Delivering on Promises

Delivering on promises means fulfilling all commitments made to clients accurately and timely.

- **What It Is:** To make certain that everything promised and committed to during the sales interaction – from ordering to delivery of the goods – actually happens.

- **Why It Matters:** Fulfilling promises builds reliability, customer trust, and loyalty.

- **Techniques:** Set realistic expectations, follow through on commitments, and provide regular updates to clients.

Example: For a client in the construction sector, this provider demonstrated a reliable service from beginning to end – they fulfilled all project deliverables and specifications in line with their commitments, leading to a high level of client satisfaction and positive reviews, which contributed to building a reputation as a trustworthy service provider.

18.7 Handling Complaints Professionally

Handling complaints professionally involves addressing issues with empathy, efficiency, and respect.

- **What It Is:** Resolving customer complaints in a respectful, timely, and effective manner.

- **Why It Matters:** When bad things happen to customers, professional complaint handling can turn lemons into lemonade, not least by strengthening their bond to you.

- **Techniques:** Listen actively, apologize sincerely, offer effective solutions, and follow up to ensure satisfaction.

Example: I helped a client develop a strong complaint processing system. Because they took significant steps to quickly and appropriately resolve complaints, their clients became more satisfied and less likely to leave. Instead, they turned potential detractors into promoters.

18.8 Creating Long-Term Value

Creating long-term value focuses on building lasting relationships with clients rather than short-term gains.

- **What It Is:** Delivering a consistently superior level of value to clients, both over the long term and through interactions across various channels, by delivering quality products and services that are supportive of the clients' objectives.

- **Why It Matters:** Value creation ultimately comes from customers – their profit and wellbeing matter, and if they don't thrive, neither will the company.

- **Techniques:** Offer ongoing support, continuously improve products, and prioritize customer success.

Example: A client whose premise and business is to create software for a better user experience presents an offer inside a very long perspective of value as they deliver innovation in form of regular updates, continuous support and exclusive experimental access to new features and ideas. That overall orientation cannot be found in traditional annual contracts – it's proven to create customer loyalty and an innovation culture that in the end drives higher lifetime value and repeat business.

18.9 Ethical Dilemmas in Sales

In sales, the classic ethical dilemma is a situation where it is not obvious what the right action is.

- **What It Is:** Facing choices that test your ethical principles and professional standards.

- **Why It Matters:** Handling ethical dilemmas correctly maintains your integrity, reputation, and client trust.

- **Techniques:** Talk to experts, reflect on your own values, judge long-term effects, pick the best of all ethically relevant factors.

Example: The client was under pressure from his boss to push a product his boss wanted to sell the client, when the client knew it would not meet the need he had. But the client said that being able to tell his boss that the competitor's product was a better fit, then turning and going to a competitor gave him the confidence that he could do the right thing, build the relationship on integrity, and trust over time, so he had a client for life (long-term relationship and referrals).

18.10 Promoting Ethical Behavior in Teams

Promoting ethical behavior in teams involves encouraging and enforcing ethical practices across the organization.

- **What It Is:** Create a culture and environment that fosters respect for honesty, integrity and ethical behaviour in your team.

- **Why It Matters:** Everyone feels invested because all members of the team are held to the same standard. You and your staff won't lose the trust and respect of your customers for the same reason you won't lose the respect of your own kids.

- **Techniques:** Develop and adopt a code of ethics, provide ongoing training, lead by example and create accountability mechanisms.

Example: One of my clients created an ethics training programme for his sales team, a business that interacted most frequently with customers. He reinforced the importance of behaving ethically, aligned the team's activities with the company mission and values, and improved team cohesion and performance.

18.11 The Impact of Ethics on Reputation

Ultimately, the role of ethics in reputation should help to reveal the ways in which ethical behaviour contributes to public perception and business success.

- **What It Is:** The effect of ethical actions by the company on how your clients, strategic partners, and the public perceive your business.

- **Why It Matters:** Good ethics help to attract clients and build trust, which are fundamental to long-term business success.

- **Techniques:** Be consistently ethical in conduct, openly proclaim your principles, and handle ethical violations swiftly.

Example: A finance client improved his company's reputation by making a public statement committing to act in an ethical manner, and demonstrating that his organisation was responsive and transparent – actions that caused other potential clients to favour them with their business, becoming more profitable and gradually taking more of the market.

18.12 Case Studies of Ethical Sales

After all, what's a better use of time than showcasing actual ethical sales cases in action, and the results?

- **What It Is:** Documenting instances where ethical behavior led to successful and positive outcomes.

- **Why It Matters:** Offers examples of unethical behavior and gives readers additional reasons to be ethical.

- **Techniques:** Publish case studies, focus on benefits of a positive standards approach, and draw on these as examples in training and messaging.

Example: One interviewee described a case study where he decided to forego an immediate sale in favour of a long-term relationship based on trust and integrity. He recommended a competitor's product to a client who needed something that his company didn't offer. That postponed a quick immediate sale, but prompted an appreciative client to do business with him in additional ways, to recommend him to others on that occasion and many times in the future, and to praise him as a company that he could count on for its honesty and integrity.

Conclusion

These chapters are dedicated to metrics and analytics, how to overcome slumps in sales, and why integrity is important when it comes to selling. With these, you will maximise your results, instil trust in your clientele, and ensure a sustainable success in high-ticket remote closing. The right metrics consistently growing, a positive mindset and an ability to adapt, and a commitment to integrity – as long as you have that, you can scale sustainably.

Chapter 19: Networking and Community Building

"Your network is your net worth." - Porter Gale

19.1 Importance of Networking

Networking is the cornerstone of professional growth and opportunity.

- **What It Is:** Establishing and nurturing relationships within your industry.

- **Why It Matters:** Networking helps you find new clients, partnerships, and points of view that can boost your career.

- **Techniques:** Attend events, engage on social media, join professional groups, and maintain regular contact.

Example: I have cultivated a network of industry contacts who are experts in their fields, and when I began my consultancy work, I attended a sales conference early in my career. As a result of my contact and networking strategy, I met several major players in the industry who benefited from my research, and I leveraged those relationships to gain high-profile collaborations that tremendously enhanced my business. One of these contacts led to a speaking engagement that improved my profile in my field.

19.2 Building Professional Relationships

Building strong professional relationships requires consistent effort and genuine interest in others.

- **What It Is:** Developing mutually beneficial connections with colleagues, clients, and industry leaders.

- **Why It Matters:** Strong relationships can lead to referrals, collaboration opportunities, and career growth.

- **Techniques:** Check in regularly with contacts; offer help; acknowledge those who have helped you; deliver on mutual commitments.

Example: One former client I maintained contact with introduced me to the vice president of technology at a major tech company. I won a consulting contract that paid me for a couple of years, and have had an ongoing relationship with that company for more than a decade, which underscores the benefits of sustained professional relationships.

19.3 Joining Industry Groups

Joining industry groups can provide access to resources, support, and networking opportunities.

- **What It Is:** Becoming a member of professional organizations relevant to your field.
- **Why It Matters:** Industry groups offer networking events, educational resources, and forums for discussion.
- **Techniques:** Actively participate in group activities, attend events, and engage with other members.

Example: Paying membership dues and joining a national sales association provided me with opportunities to access conference events and reference materials, which kept me up to speed on industry trends, as well as opportunities to share my knowledge, which resulted in speaking engagements and new client referrals.

19.4 Attending Conferences

Attending conferences is an excellent way to network, learn, and showcase your expertise.

- **What It Is:** Participating in industry-specific conferences and events.

- **Why It Matters:** Conferences provide opportunities to meet potential clients, partners, and mentors.

- **Techniques:** Do your homework, talk to people, tell them you may follow up, make a panel or workshop.

Example: At a sales technology conference, I attended sessions to learn new techniques and network with others in the industry. I formed valuable partnerships, learned about new sales tools for my business, and even learned how to negotiate better deals with my suppliers. I was able to apply the knowledge and connections I gained to increase my annual revenue by 15 per cent.

19.5 Leveraging Social Media

Using social media helps you increase your network and further your personal branding at a greater level.

- **What It Is:** Making use of platforms such as LinkedIn, Twitter, and Facebook to network with industry professionals.

- **Why It Matters:** Social media enables you to remain relevant in the public eye, share ideas, and potentially make new connections with prospective clients.

- **Techniques:** Post regularly, share important info, 'like' or comment on other people's posts, and join groups.

Example: I grew my LinkedIn network substantially, made many new contacts, and became known as an expert in remote closing. It also resulted in speaking engagements, requests to collaborate with other experts, and new client inquiries.

19.6 Creating Content

You might very well be creating the best content in your area – producing work that you feel could qualify you as an expert in the field, and win you a loyal audience to boot.

- **What It Is:** Producing articles, videos, podcasts, and other content relevant to your industry.

- **Why It Matters:** Thoughtful, well-executed content showcases your expertise, attracting prospects and collaborators.

- **Techniques:** Identify your audience's needs, create engaging content, and promote it across platforms.

Example: I began writing a blog on remote sales techniques, sharing examples, tips, and methodology. I gained further online visibility, via a link to the blog, and the subsequent clients helped to build a track record of expertise and experience. This in turn led to opportunities for guest blogs on established industry sites.

19.7 Engaging with Your Community

Engaging with your community builds strong connections and fosters a sense of belonging.

- **What It Is:** Actively participating in discussions, forums, and events within your professional community.

- **Why It Matters:** Engagement keeps you informed, builds relationships, and enhances your visibility.

- **Techniques:** Comment on posts, participate in discussions, support community initiatives, and host meet-ups.

Example: I participated in online forums for salespeople where I provided tips and tricks and even answered others' questions. As a result of being a helpful and knowledgeable resource, I got more referrals, expanded my network, and ended up with more clients.

19.8 Collaboration Opportunities

Collaboration can open new doors and enhance your projects through shared expertise and resources.

- **What It Is:** Working with other professionals or companies on joint projects.

- **Why It Matters:** Collaborations can lead to innovation, extend reach and generate new business opportunities.

- **Techniques:** Identify potential collaborators, propose mutually beneficial projects, and maintain clear communication.

Example: I recently teamed up with a marketing expert on a webinar series on our remote closing strategy. The joint venture gave both of us access to each other's audiences and allowed both of us to tap into each other's area of expertise. The outcome of this venture was wildly successful: I gained new clients from the venture, as did my partner, and we both came away from the event with greater credibility in our industries.

19.9 Hosting Events and Webinars

It also gives you the chance to host events and webinars, which puts your company front and centre and allows you to connect directly with your market.

- **What It Is:** Organizing and leading industry-related events, both online and offline.

- **Why It Matters:** Events and webinars give you a platform to share your knowledge, network, and establish authority.

- **Techniques:** Plan engaging topics, promote your events, and follow up with attendees.

Example: I delivered a webinar series on leading-edge remote closing methodologies. The webinars attracted a global audience, boosted my brand, and earned me several new consulting contracts. The events also dedicated time for audience feedback and insights.

19.10 Mentorship and Coaching

Mentorship and coaching can accelerate your professional growth and help others develop their skills.

- **What It Is:** Building relationships where experienced professionals guide less experienced individuals.

- **Why It Matters:** Mentorship enhances learning by offering mentees knowledge, advice, and networking opportunities and making mentors learn how to become mentors.

- **Techniques:** Seek mentors, offer to mentor others, and engage in regular, meaningful interactions.

Example: I coached a junior sales professional on closing high-ticket sales. After several regular coaching sessions over several months, he was able to close more sales and was rewarded with a promotion. It also helped me to significantly boost my own coaching skills and expand my network.

19.11 Networking Etiquette

Networking etiquette involves respectful and professional behavior that fosters positive interactions.

- **What It Is:** The principles and practices of courteous and effective networking.

- **Why It Matters:** Good etiquette ensures positive, lasting impressions and strong professional relationships.

- **Techniques:** Be timely, respond quickly, give the appearance of being sincerely interested, and give without the expectation of return.

Example: After a few years of always 'networking the right way' (returning calls, sending thank-you notes and following up with people), I built a trustworthy network of people willing to work with me and to refer clients to me that could help me maintain a good name.

19.12 Building a Personal Brand

Building a personal brand differentiates you and establishes your unique value in the industry.

- **What It Is:** Cultivating an occupation-specific, genuine professional identity rooted in your competencies, values, and knowledge.

- **Why It Matters:** A good personal brand attracts opportunities, can build your credibility, and help on your path to professional growth.

- **Techniques:** Brand yourself; be consistent (develop an 'elevator speech'); be everywhere (get quoted and cited).

Example: Separating my personal brand – a remote closing expert – from Western Union and sending out messages through blogs, social media, and speaking events about what it took for me to succeed put me in a position to ultimately be hired as a sophisticated closer – and to be a speaker on the subject. These speaking arrangements and well-known clients reinforced my credibility.

Chapter 20: Future Trends in Remote Closing

"The future belongs to those who prepare for it today." - Malcolm X

20.1 Emerging Technologies

Emerging technologies are transforming how remote closing is conducted, offering new tools and efficiencies.

- **What It Is:** Taking advantage of new AI, machine learning, and advanced analytics to jumpstart or turbocharge sales processes.

- **Why It Matters:** Staying updated with technology helps you remain competitive and improve efficiency.

- **Techniques:** Experiment with new tools, invest in technologies, and train your team on them.

Example: I assisted a client to incorporate AI-powered CRM tools that provided live input and predictive analytics on their buyers, providing their sales team with unprecedented insights that allowed them to tailor the pitches and significantly boost conversion rates by 25 per cent, with machine learning finding hidden patterns in buyer behaviour.

20.2 Changes in Buyer Behavior

Understanding changes in buyer behavior is crucial for adapting your sales strategies.

- **What It Is:** Shifts in how customers make purchasing decisions and what they value.

- **Why It Matters:** Adapting to how buyers behave will help you keep your sales strategies relevant.

- **Techniques:** Conduct ongoing market research, get customer feedback, track results and adjust accordingly.

Example: I tracked the trend and found that buyers were wanting a more considered and personal approach to selling. We adapted our sales process and included more tailored proposals and follow-up for better engagement. We created and worked with customer surveys and focus groups for continued adaptation to new trends, maintaining 100 per cent customer satisfaction.

20.3 Impact of AI and Automation

AI and automation are revolutionizing remote closing by streamlining processes and enhancing decision-making.

- **What It Is:** Deploying AI, robots, and other automated systems to perform tasks and analyze data that are replicable and repetitive.

- **Why It Matters:** More efficient, less error-prone, and deeper sales performance insights.

- **Techniques:** Use a chatbot to field all initial customer requests, employ AI-guided lead scoring, and auto-send follow-up emails.

Example: One client adopted an AI-driven lead scoring system to identify budding high-potential leads. This automated process meant that the salespeople could then spend more time curating sales for the best prospects, and our conversion rate increased by 20 per cent. We also automated more standard emails, which generated more time to do more clever work.

20.4 Evolving Sales Techniques

Sales techniques are continually evolving to meet new challenges and opportunities in the market.

- **What It Is:** New approaches to opening and closing sales with customers.

- **Why It Matters:** Staying on top of emerging techniques and practices makes sure your approach to sales is current and cutting-edge.

- **Techniques:** Stay updated with industry trends, attend training sessions, and experiment with new strategies.

Example: With a sales team that I taught the Challenger Sales Model (teach, tailor, take control), we tapped into their clients' needs better and significantly improved their sales. Their ability to continually train and then adapt to new strategies allowed them to stay ahead of the curve.

20.5 Virtual Reality in Sales

Virtual reality (VR) is a technological tool that has the power to enhance sales pitches and interaction.

- **What It Is:** Using VR technology to create immersive sales experiences.

- **Why It Matters:** Innovative VR offers a creative way to demonstrate products and services in a dynamic way that will engage customers.

- **Techniques:** Develop VR presentations, create virtual product demos, and offer immersive client experiences.

Example: Our real estate client used this technology for their site visitors to showcase properties virtually and help them make faster decisions and engage better by experiencing their asset remotely. We increased interest and reduced the sales cycle by offering a unique experience.

20.6 Sustainability and Sales

Sustainability is becoming increasingly important in sales as consumers and businesses prioritize environmental responsibility.

- **What It Is:** Integrating sustainable practices into your sales strategy and operations.

- **Why It Matters:** Whether you want to improve your image or attract new business by offering green products and services, you can make your business more sustainable.

- **Techniques:** Showcase important sustainable attributes of your items; implement green operations and publicize your corporate sustainability efforts.

Example: A client in the packaging industry wanted to improve his business and attract new customers. I suggested focusing on the recyclable materials he was using and the sustainability of his business model. This approach worked well, and his business saw an increase in environmentally conscious clients. The company also accomplished some green initiatives and improved the corporate image and employee morale.

20.7 Global Market Trends

Understanding global market trends is essential for adapting your sales strategies to international markets.

- **What It Is:** Staying abreast of the flux of economics, culture, and technology worldwide that affect global markets.

- **Why It Matters:** Staying sensitive to global changes allows you to take advantage of new opportunities and minimize risk.

- **Techniques:** Conduct market research, monitor international news, and adapt your strategies accordingly.

Example: A client broadened her business into emerging markets by changing its sales process to fit local consumer tastes and economic conditions, successfully entering these markets and growing sales significantly. We developed a message that would overcome cultural differences and establish emotional resonance with prospective customers.

20.8 Preparing for the Future

As part of planning, it is better to imagine the future as different from the past and to provide your team with the abilities and tools they will require.

- **What It Is:** Developing strategies and plans to adapt to future trends and challenges.

- **Why It Matters:** Staying ahead of your competition and weathering storms of change.

- **Techniques:** Constant learning – stay up to date on events that might affect your line of work and plan for different possibilities.

Example: We developed a future-proofing plan for a client that included biannual refresher training courses on emerging technologies and new market trends, while also having contingency plans for any potential market disruptions that might impact their business.

20.9 Adapting to Remote Work

People need to grow accustomed to working from home since all companies will be remote due to its flexibility and more efficiency.

- **What It Is:** Adjusting your operations and strategies to support a remote workforce.

- **Why It Matters:** Ensures productivity, collaboration, and employee satisfaction in a remote setting.

- **Techniques:** Implement remote collaboration tools, establish clear communication protocols, and support work-life balance.

Example: A client had a sales team that was fully remote post-pandemic. They maintained productivity and team morale through clear, regular communications over virtual avenues and regular one-on-one check-ins. This resulted in achieving projected sales numbers while building procedures and best practices for remote work.

20.10 Digital Transformation

Digital transformation is about leveraging technology to enhance every aspect of your sales process.

- **What It Is:** Using technology in new ways to improve operations and customer experiences.

- **Why It Matters:** Enhances efficiency, accuracy, and competitiveness in the market.

- **Techniques:** Implement CRM systems, use data analytics, and adopt digital marketing strategies.

Example: I helped a client achieve digital transformation with the implementation of a new CRM system that integrated all customer data and automated customer administration processes. The client achieved greater efficiency through targeted and personalized customer interaction, leading to a 30 per cent increase in customer satisfaction and a revenue boost of nearly 15 per cent.

20.11 The Role of Data in Future Sales

Data will play an increasingly crucial role in driving sales strategies and decision-making.

- **What It Is:** Collecting, analyzing, and leveraging data to inform sales strategies and operations.

- **Why It Matters:** Data-driven decisions are more accurate and effective, leading to better outcomes.

- **Techniques:** Employ 'big data' analytics tools, track the appropriate key performance indicators in detail, and tune in to better ways of doing things based on the results of those analyses.

Example: Using data analytics, we helped identify the most profitable customer segments for one of the clients and tailored the marketing messaging accordingly, resulting in improved marketing ROI and sales conversion rates. By continuously monitoring sales data and analyzing its variations over time, we ensured their strategies aligned with market trends and shopper preferences.

20.12 Innovating for Tomorrow

Innovation is essential for staying competitive and addressing future challenges in remote closing.

- **What It Is:** Coming up with new ideas, products, and strategies for staying one step ahead.

- **Why It Matters:** Continuous innovation drives growth, improves efficiency, and meets evolving customer needs.

- **Techniques:** Create a culture of innovation, invest in R&D, and get your team to think creatively.

Example: Seeing that they were creative outside of work, I encouraged a client to set up a separate space (an innovation lab) where his employees could innovate new ways of using sales channels and technologies. This led to several breakthrough ideas that improved their sales process and offered richer customer experiences. We also correlated that with multistage brainstorming sessions to continue the innovation momentum.

Conclusion

These chapters provide key tips on how to stay on the pulse of networking, building a community, and setting yourself up for future closing success. What do you need to do to ensure continued growth, evolution, and revenue in remote closing? Put these tips into action to survive these times and persevere in high-ticket remote closing. These chapters will provide actionable takes and tips for you to revolutionize your trajectory in remote and digitally enabled progress. Arm yourself with the tools necessary to not only ride out this storm of change, but thrive through the unexpected and the new.

Conclusion

Wow. What a journey we've been on together! I hope it has been as eye-opening for you as it has been for me. Having covered every aspect of high-ticket remote closing and sales from the basics to the more advanced stuff, you now have a toolbox full of ways you can benefit from being a remote closer and help others do the same. Let's quickly summarise what we've covered in each chapter, reinforce those teachings, and then bring everything together to demonstrate how you, too, can become a seven-figure remote closer.

Conclusion: Mastering High-Ticket Remote Closing

So as you wrap up this ultimate high-ticket remote closing bible, here's a recap: selling high-tier remote closing involves mastering a sophisticated set of sales techniques, as well as life lessons backed by scientific evidence and industry-specific strategies. It is a huge step, but if you have read until here and conquered the twenty chapters above, you are now better equipped as a closer to succeed not only this week, but also for a lifetime.

Chapter Summaries and Key Takeaways

Chapter 1: Understanding High-Ticket Sales

High-ticket sales are a game unto their own which requires different tactics, a different therapeutic approach, and even more value-centric thinking than most of your typical sales interactions.

Chapter 2: The Psychology of Selling

Understanding the psychology of selling is a way to relate more empathetically with clients, forge a connection, and motivate them to buy.

Chapter 3: Building a Winning Mindset

Maintaining an optimistic outlook and having a strong sense of resilience is essential for finding ways to reach your goals in an environment that is filled with risk and potential rejection.

Chapter 4: Effective Communication Skills

Good control of your techniques of communication means that your audience hears your message in a way that's both compelling and appropriate to their needs and tastes.

Chapter 5: Lead Generation Strategies

Wide-ranging lead generation methods, from content marketing to cold outreach, will build your pipeline of leads.

Chapter 6: Crafting the Perfect Pitch

Aside from knowing your audience, a solid pitch employs a clear structure, in which a benefits-led introduction is followed by a content-rich middle and a persuasive conclusion.

Chapter 7: Building and Maintaining Client Relationships

If you want to excel in the high-ticket selling game in the long term, it is vital that you cultivate and maintain long-lasting, trust-infused relationships with your clients.

Chapter 8: Advanced Closing Strategies

Advanced techniques, including the assumptive close and the urgency close, will ensure you'll close with every prospect that you want to sell.

Chapter 9: Overcoming Objections

By responding to objections with sympathy, reasonable solutions, and data-based answers, you can turn a potential stumbling block into a chance for deeper conversation.

Chapter 10: High-Ticket Case Studies

Real-life case studies and examples provide a solid training base and a useful real-world grounding in what high-ticket tactics actually look like and how to implement them.

Chapter 11: Personal Development and Mindset

Investing in knowledge, education, and experiences in all areas of life enables a more holistic approach to work and professional success.

Chapter 12: High-Ticket Remote Closing in Different Industries

Because of this, your approach to sales will need to be tailored to the subtleties of each individual industry, all of which can have a significant impact on how you formulate your own method.

Chapter 13: Lead Generation Strategies

To execute an effective lead generation plan, which combines content marketing, social media, and paid advertising, you will want to build your accounts.

Chapter 14: Crafting the Perfect Pitch

It can help to create a concise pitch that covers the main benefits of whatever you are selling, including notes on visual aids and potential objections. Then you can build on that as people respond.

Chapter 15: Scaling Your Business

Growing your business means staffing up for sales, getting more automated, and going after your market it through different channels.

Chapter 16: Metrics and Analytics

By tracking key sales metrics and analyzing the data, you gain perceptive insights into what does work – and what doesn't – ensuring you're able to make continual improvements.

Chapter 17: Overcoming Sales Slumps

Figuring out why sales fell and having specific action steps geared to pick up the pieces puts you back on pace, and out of the doldrums once more.

Chapter 18: Ethical Selling Practices

When you sell ethically, you will earn the trust of your clients, gain a positive reputation, and establish lasting relationships with them.

Chapter 19: Networking and Community Building

Forging a professional network and becoming a member of your community helps to create bountiful avenues and opportunities for collaboration.

Chapter 20: Future Trends in Remote Closing

By paying attention to emerging market trends and anticipating where the industry is heading – such as the rise of artificial intelligence and automation, virtual reality, and sustainability – you will position yourself and your business for additional successes in the changing world of remote closing.

Final Thoughts

Skilful remote closing of high-ticket clients is a life-long practice of learning, adaptation, and growing. By following the lessons of these 20 chapters while you work your craft, you will be better prepared to engage in the intricacies of high-ticket closings, create long-lasting client partnerships, and soar to even greater heights!

Just remember, it's your ability to stay in-the-know, your flexibility, and your unrelenting focus on value that will hold the line on your ability to succeed in high-ticket remote closing. As you apply the principles and practices in this article, you will both improve your sales and earn the reputation of being a trusted, ethical, effective sales professional.

Well done! And thanks for coming along with me on that ride. Cheers for remaining in this high-paying remote closing space.

www.ingramcontent.com/pod-product-compliance
Lightning Source LLC
Chambersburg PA
CBHW082203220526
45470CB00010B/3033